The Book of The Cinque Ports 1984
has been published as a
Limited Edition of which this is

Number   2 14

A complete list of the original
subscribers is printed at the
back of the book

THE BOOK OF THE CINQUE PORTS

Who names us SANK,
and not our SINK,
Is foreigner
and foe.
His ship to be engaged,
and after bloody battle,
SUNK.
No prisoner to be taken.

Paraphrase on an old jingle recited by
a venerable Hastings Portsman.

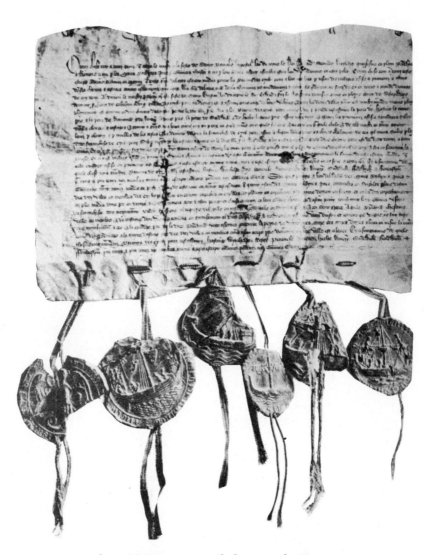

A financial agreement made between the Ports at a Brodhull held at Romney on 11 June 1392. The final paragraph reads: 'In testimony whereof we the aforesaid Barons of the Cinque Ports, to wit, Hastings, Winchelsea, Rye, Pevensea, Romney, Hythe, Dover, Sandwich, Fordwich and Faversham, for us, and for all our limbs, have appended to this written indenture, our common seals.'

THE BOOK OF THE CINQUE PORTS

Their Origin and Development, Heyday and Decline

THE PRESENT MEMBERS: HASTINGS, NEW ROMNEY,
HYTHE, DOVER AND SANDWICH; WINCHELSEA AND
RYE; DEAL, FAVERSHAM, FOLKESTONE, LYDD,
MARGATE, RAMSGATE AND TENTERDEN

BY

IVAN GREEN BA FCCEd

BARRACUDA BOOKS LIMITED
BUCKINGHAM, ENGLAND
MCMLXXXIV

PUBLISHED BY BARRACUDA BOOKS LIMITED
BUCKINGHAM, ENGLAND
AND PRINTED BY
BURGESS & SONS LIMITED
ABINGDON, ENGLAND

BOUND BY
GREEN STREET BINDERY LIMITED
OXFORD, ENGLAND

JACKET PRINTED BY
CHENEY & SONS LIMITED
BANBURY, OXON

LITHOGRAPHY BY
SOUTH MIDLANDS LITHOPLATES LIMITED
LUTON, ENGLAND

DISPLAY SET IN BASKERVILLE AND
TEXT SET IN 10/11pt BASKERVILLE BY
BEDFORDSHIRE GRAPHICS LIMITED
BEDFORD, ENGLAND

© IVAN GREEN 1984

ISBN 0 86023 209 3

Contents

Acknowledgements

In the production of this book I am indebted to many organisations and individuals for their help, and for permission to use material they have shown me. It is now my pleasant duty to thank them all, and to hope that they will enjoy the book to which they have so willingly contributed. My grateful thanks, then, to Barracuda Books Ltd, for commissioning and publishing it, and to Clive Birch for all his professional advice and assistance and that of his hard-working and long-suffering staff.

My thanks also to go Mr Ian Gill, LLB, The Registrar and Seneschal of the Cinque Ports, for all his help and interest, and for writing the Foreword; to the District Councillors, and the Town Mayors of the Ports and their Members, and to their helpful staffs; to the Sussex, Essex, and Kent County Libraries, especially those of Seaford, Hastings, Rye, Tenterden, Hythe, Folkestone, Dover, Deal, Sandwich, Faversham, Margate, Brightlingsea and Great Yarmouth; to the Dover Harbour Board, and to many museums, especially those of Hastings, Winchelsea, Lydd, Tenterden, Folkestone, Dover, Deal, Sandwich Town Hall, Faversham Fleur De Lis Heritage Centre, and those of Great Yarmouth; to many individuals, and especially to Mrs Sylvia Corrall, Miss Mary Ward, Messrs Ray Warner, Ian Waters, Edward Gilders, W. Roberts, R.I. Pritchard, Cllr Marie Hart, Cllr W.H. Robertson, Doctor Richard Stevens and Mrs Mary Stevens, and Col Reeves who, in his period of voluntary duty at the Winchelsea Museum, introduced me to many treasures, especially the fine collection of town seals there, which otherwise I should certainly have missed.

Over the years many people have allowed me to see and to copy treasured pictures and documents they owned, and it is particularly regretted that limitations of space prohibits the reproduction of them all.

Many of these were reproductions, or copies of originals, whose origin and present ownership are unknown to me. Others have changed hands, finding new homes in public and private collections, museums and archives. It would be an impossible task to trace the history of every illustration and document so that individual thanks and credit could be offered in each case. I should therefore like to thank them all collectively.

Of the many helpers there is not space to thank individually, I express my regret for the ommissions, and record my sincere thanks and appreciation here. Thank you, everyone.

Foreword

by Ian G. Gill LLB, Registrar & Seneschal, Cinque Ports

The Installation of Her Majesty Queen Elizabeth the Queen Mother as Lord Warden of the Cinque Ports at Dover on 1 August 1979, not only marked an important step in the history of the Cinque Ports, but also led to a regeneration of interest in the Cinque Ports themselves. Enquiries for information are now regularly received from throughout Britain and, indeed, the world.

Mr Green's book is particularly timely, as it will help to meet this renewed curiousity about the role of the Cinque Ports.

The uniqueness of the Cinque Ports lies not just in that it formed the nucleus of a Navy in order to protect the coast from invasion and maintain the freedom of sea passage, but also that, unlike so many historical institutions, it has stoutly defended its position and, in spite of many constitutional and other changes, protects its heritage with pride.

Mr Green's book sets out that heritage.

The Cinque Ports sign placed at the entrance to each Cinque Port town. The arms are those used by the Lord Warden and, with small modifications, by most of the member towns.

ABOVE: The fishermens' quarters at Hastings, with the old net shops. The church shown is the old Fishermens' Church, but is now a museum. BELOW: The municipal buildings and the New Inn in New Romney's main street. The prefix 'new' is modern, to distinguish the town from 'old' Romney.

Birth of the Confederation

In early times the coasts of SE England were the scene of frequent landings by wandering bands, by colonisers, by full-scale invading forces, and indeed by whole armies. The Romans themselves invaded the country by means of landings on these shores as later did the Northmen, intent at first on pillage and rapine and later, on conquest.

In spite of many attempts, no permanent solution was discovered. Even the powerful Roman empire with its coastal defensive fortresses, its mobile army units and its Classis Britannica, was sometimes gravely embarrassed, and when the Empire declined there was no effective barrier of any kind for several centuries. Later, the burgh system, in which a town was made responsible for its own defence in return for a measure of self-government, worked quite well for populous areas, but the many attempts made to buy off raiders only resulted in their certain, and early, return. Many other efforts, such as those of King Alfred, and of Aethelred in 1008 were shortlived, and the later system of hiring mercenaries to supplement the King's ships was both uncertain in its reliability and unsatisfactory, since they of necessity spent their time waiting, and raiders soon learnt to avoid their areas.

This was not difficult since communications were poor, slow, or non-existent, and raiding parties could land, do their nefarious work, and be gone before any effective defence could even be arranged, let alone put into action.

In the reign of Edward the Confessor, about the year 1050, the mercenary system was abandoned, at least in SE England, and was replaced by Ship Service. This was really a reintroduction of the old burgh system in a new guise, in that seaport towns in East Sussex and Kent which, in geographical sequence from west to east were Hastings, Romney, Hythe, Dover and Sandwich, became responsible for provision of ships and men for the service of the Crown, in return for a considerable degree of self-government. They all had harbours and possessed seaworthy fishing fleets, manned by skilful crews well used to navigating the difficult and stormy narrow sea separating England from the continent of Europe.

The degree of autonomy which could be granted to each town unfortunately differed according to the rights in them already held by other organisations, most of them ecclesiastical.

For instance, many rights in Sandwich had already been granted years before by King Canute to Christ Church Canterbury, and it was not until 1364 that they were fully claimed by Edward III.

The Archbishop of Canterbury continued to hold some rights in Romney and Hythe.

It is fortunate that details of this ship service are recorded in the Domesday Book entries of several of the towns, but it is sad to realise that there is no entry at all for Hastings, which was an important Saxon town and harbour, and which would certainly have formed part of the original organisation.

Domesday Book, completed in 1086, actually covers three distinct periods extending over twenty years in all, recording the holders of property before the Conquest, to whom it passed at the redistribution of lands carried out by William of Normandy, and who held in in 1086.

From what evidence there is, it seems that the position of the Ports was unchanged, and that the Conqueror simply confirmed the Portsmen in the duties and privileges they possessed before his invasion in 1066.

This perhaps is not surprising, because William needed the service of the Ports more than they needed him since, if he could hold their loyalty, his position in the country, and his lifeline to Normandy, were alike fairly secure. If he lost their loyalty and their services passed to an enemy, then he was in peril indeed.

The most complete entry in Domesday Book is that for Dover, and the translation (*Victoria County History*) reads:

'The burgesses supplied the king once in the year 20 ships for 15 days, and in each ship were 21 men. This [service] they did because he had remitted to them the sac and soc'.

The Romney record, after listing the Archbishop's previously granted rights already mentioned reads:

'- - - but the king has all the service due from them, and they themselves have all dues and other fines, in return for service on the sea, and they are in the king's hands'.

Hythe's service, recorded in Domesday Monachorum, because as previously mentioned, the church had rights there, reads:

'- - - and there belonged and [still] belong 21 burgesses of whom the king has sea service, and therefore they are quit [of dues] through all England - - -'.

'Sandwic - - - is a lathe and hundred in itself, and pays the king sea service like Dover'.

As is seen, the service was for 15 days a year free of cost to the King, and a further 15 days at his cost if he needed them. There were, however, many later occasions when this service was considerably extended, sometimes into several months, and the matter of payment was also honoured in the breach.

The Portsmens' service was threefold in character: the repelling of sudden incursions by seaborne marauding bands, for which their geographical position and local knowledge was invaluable; the naval service both for defensive and for offensive operations initiated by the King, when they were often part of a larger force in which the King's own ships and those impressed for the purpose from western and eastern ports sometimes also took part; and the transporting of the King, his household, his officials and his armed forces, to and from the continent as need arose.

Since most of these operations, except the large scale naval encounters, were of fairly short duration, the 15 days' service at the King's cost and 15 at the Portsmens' costs, were probably fairly adequate.

From Domesday Book it is not possible to compute the number of ships and men the ports supplied to the King, since the recorded details are too fragmentary and incomplete, but in later charters it was stated to be 57 ships, with crews of 20 or 21 men, with a captain and sometimes also a boy.

The number of ships and crews provided by the various ports varied from time to time, according to the service required and to the condition of the ports. Sometimes, for instance, French raids, or storms, or harbour problems, made the response from any one port impossible.

Later too, when ships were getting much bigger, the small Cinque Port ships were not so much needed, and the Portsmen were then sometimes ordered to supply fewer ships but with double crews, the surplus men, being skilled mariners particularly knowledgeable in the tides and currents of the narrow seas, being of enormous value in reinforcing the crews of the King's ships, and those he impressed.

There is however a clear and full statement of the ship service of the Ports in the 13th century in the charter of Edward I, (translated here by Edward Knocker in his book *An Account of the Grand Court of Shepway* published in 1862).

'These are the services which the Barons of the Cinque Ports owe to our Lord the King from yeare to yeare by Sea, if need be; that is to wit, the Towne of Hastings, three ships; the Lowey of Pevensey, one ship; Bulvarhithe and Petit Hiam, one ship; Beakesborne, in Kent, one ship; Grenocle, in Kent, two men with two anchors, with the ships of Hastings; the Towne of Rye, five ships; the Towne of Winchelsea, tenne ships; the Port of Romney and Old Romney, foure ships; Lydde, one ship; the Port of Hithe, five ships; the Porte of Dover, ninteene ships;

Folston, one ship; the Towne of Feversham, one ship; the Porte of Sandwich, Stonor, Fordwiche, Dale, and Sarre, five ships.

'The Summe Totale, fifty-seven ships.

'And it is to wit, that when the King will have his service of the aforesaid ships they shall have forty Daies of Summons, and shall find to the King in every ship twenty men and a master, and the manner of every ship is to be armed and furnished for to do the Service of the King. And the ships shall be fitted at the proper costs of the Cinque Ports when they shall be summoned.

'And when the ships shall have tarried fifteen daies in the Service of the King, at the proper costs of the Cinque Ports; and after the fifteen daies past they tarry not, but at the costs of the King, if he have to do, that is to wit, the Master of the ship shall take for a day Six Pence, the Constable six Pence, and every of the others Three Pence'.

ABOVE: The fine 18th century town hall at Hythe. OPPOSITE ABOVE: A panoramic view of Dover, from the Western Heights. LEFT: The Sandwich Guildhall. A mainly 16th century building containing many items of historical interest, it has been altered somewhat externally, and an extension, not shown here, has been added to the end adjacent to the market. RIGHT: The Strand Gate at Winchelsea, one of the original gates to the old walled town. BELOW: Rye Harbour. This is one of the few Cinque Port towns still possessing a harbour.

ABOVE: An old view of Hastings, looking eastwards.
BELOW: A mid-19th century drawing of the fishermens' quarter at Hastings.

16

Heyday of the Ports

As far as the King was concerned, the early days of his fleet of the south-eastern ports and harbours were inauspicious, since in 1052 Earl Godwin returned from his banishment in Flanders and it is recorded that: 'having already won over the Sussex garrison and mariners of Hastings', he visited Pevensey, Dungeness, Romney, Hythe, Folkestone, Dover and Sandwich, with which towns he had close ties, and mustered from them a fleet with which he sailed up the Thames Estuary to London, where he was opposed by a Royal fleet of fifty sail and the King's army.

King Edward, at first obdurate, found he could trust neither his armed troops nor his own Royal naval fleet, and was therefore forced to come to terms with Godwin. However, the ships of the ports which had opposed him then formed part of his fleet during his campaign in Wales in 1063 under Earl Harold who, having subdued the rising there, brought back two trophies to present to the King, the head of Gruffydd the leader of the rebellion and the beak of that man's warship.

In the fateful year of 1066, the Cinque Ports fleet was again in action, this time sailing up the East coast in support of King Harold in his campaign against Tostig and the invading Hardrada, King of Norway. Within a few days of its successful end, William of Normandy had landed in Sussex, unopposed at sea because the Cinque Ports ships were still on the North-east coast supporting King Harold, the remainder returning homewards, provisionless and unfit to take further offensive action. Had the Portsmen been at their home stations, there is little doubt that their ships would have wrought fearful havoc on William's heavily laden transports before they had reached land.

After the battle of Hastings, William marched eastwards, taking a fearful revenge on the people of Romney, who had badly mauled a Norman squadron, which had either accidentally or mistakenly come ashore there, before entering Dover. Accounts of the takings of Dover vary. Some writers assert that the town was voluntarily surrendered, others that after a short siege he took the castle, afterwards beheading the Saxon commander, Ashburnham and his son at the castle gateway. All accounts agree on the dreadful behaviour of his troops, who committed murder, rape, robbery and violence of all kinds before burning the town to the ground, activities which did little to commend him to the Portsmen.

However, the town was rapidly rebuilt and William, realising that he needed the Portsmen more than they needed him, was most accommodating in his arrangements for his newly conquered Kingdom. He confirmed the pre-Conquest charters of the Portsmen who, unlike most of the conquered Saxons, seem to have lost nothing from his invasion. Their loyalty was of course of crucial importance to him, since they were in the position of securing, or placing in peril, the crossing of the Dover Strait, his lifeline with his lands and base on the continent.

For their part, the Portsmen seem to have accepted the position and three years later, in 1069, they took to sea, when a strong Danish raiding fleet was driven off from Dover and Sandwich with heavy losses.

Their more peaceful occupations of fishing, maintaining commercial links with European ports and, especially in the case of Hastings and the eastern ports, principally Sandwich and Dover, the transporting of great officers of state and church, and of men and goods across the Channel went on, interrupted from time to time by calls to perform their official maritime service to the Crown, and the less official engagement with, and the chasing away of, piratical seaborne groups, mostly from Northern Europe.

Of their later, discreditable actions of piracy, robbery on the high seas, and bloody raids on European ports, there is no record as early as this, though it is quite possible that any such early records have long since disappeared. Certainly, much idea of combined action at sea, in the modern sense, was unknown, and when the Portsmen, either in their official or unofficial capacity set out as a group against enemy ships, it was a case of the commander of each ship selecting independently an enemy ship which he could engage, without much thought of any combined strategy. That was to come much later.

Disasters, such as the loss of the fleet in the Scottish expedition of 1091 in a great storm, caused severe reductions for the Cinque Port towns of both men and ships. The men were of course irreplaceable, but new little ships could be built quite quickly on the open beaches of all the ports. Shipbuilding was mostly a communal activity and the skills required, most of them fairly simple, were passed down from generation to generation, and among men to whom it was not their living.

The important fishing industry continued, though today, with our enormous variety of food culled from all over the world, it is difficult to realise the importance of fish in the diet of our forefathers who ate much less, if indeed any, red meat. Enormous quantities of fish were then consumed, especially in religious establishments, where the good life in food and wine was enjoyed.

It is probable that the yearly fish fair at Yarmouth was well established at the end of the 11th century, though its origins remain undiscovered.

In the 12th century, despite the ports being involved in the 'desultry dynastic wars of the period' and of carrying the protagonists to and fro across the Channel, there was in the main little need for large assemblies of ships of war, though there were many occasions when the Portsmen were required to perform their service, sometimes to repel piratical raiders and at others to ferry the King and his men to and from Normandy. Cinque Ports ships took a major part in the crusading fleet which captured Lisbon from the Moors in 1147, and a further involvement in crusading occurred in 1190 when, of the total of about a hundred ships which carried Richard I's crusaders, no less than one third were from the Ports. Sir James Ramsey noted that, since they were paid by the year, they must have been additional to those required for the normal ship service to the Crown.

For most of the 12th century the Channel became an Anglo-Norman sea, a great bridge between two communities sharing the same sovereign, and offensive action was in general as limited in that century as it was to be extensive and violent in the next.

The fishing industry went on apace, and the great Yarmouth Herring Fair had by now become well established and formalised. Of their other great privilege, honours at court, it is recorded that the barons were in London to carry their canopy over King Richard (Coeur de Lion) at his coronation in 1189.

It was a century, too, when many of the towns were granted charters, either new ones to reinforce or replace old ones, or initial charters to regularise and acknowledge the position the recipient towns had held less officially during previous years. Among others, charters were granted to Fordwich in 1111 by Henry I, to Rye, Winchelsea, Sandwich and Hythe in 1155, and to Lydd in 1156 by Henry II. The same King granted a second charter to Fordwich, then the port for Canterbury.

Later in the century Rye and Winchelsea, both of which had previously been joined to Hastings, received their own charters and assumed full status as head ports, the title of the organisation thenceforth becoming 'The Cinque Ports and the Two Antient Towns'.

In the 13th century, often known as 'the violent century', the Cinque Ports reached almost their peak of power, becoming so important, and indeed so essential to the Crown, that effective action to restrain their violence, their bloody quarrels, their piracy, wrecking, and robbery on the high seas, was impossible to carry out. They were undeniably superb seamen, they operated in their own home-built little ships, which were more speedy and handleable than those of their opponents, and they were brave to a degree, even reckless, often engaging and defeating ships both bigger and much more numerous than their own.

The primary cause of the violence was the loss by England of Normandy in 1204, thus transforming the Channel and the Straits, which for years had been virtually an Anglo-Norman lake, a bridge between two countries serving the same Royal house, into England's moat, her first line of defence and the corridor for her attacks on continental targets. Added to this was the struggle between King and barons, and a general atmosphere of violence and the glorification of war for its own sake. As early in the century as 1202 the Portsmen were at sea in force against the French, as they were to be on many subsequent occasions. A number of important charters confirming their many privileges and rights were granted to the Ports in 1205, the year after the loss of Normandy, doubtless to remind them of their vastly increased responsibilities in view of the risk of large-scale war with France.

In the spring of 1208 the Cinque Port ships were ordered to return to their home ports so as to be ready to join the King's fleet for war in the summer, and they were also instructed to select some of their most competent men to serve in the King's own ships, where their detailed knowledge of the narrow seas, with their tide rips, their currents and their danger areas would be of great value. The King also appreciated their superb seamanship, learned during a lifetime spent in frail craft in dangerous waters.

In 1209 Yarmouth, by this time already a prosperous and important town which had outgrown, both in size and in commercial importance, the little towns of the Ports, was made a free borough, with all the accompanying rights and privileges. Henceforth there were to be centuries of quarrelling and disagreement between the town and the Portsmen, the increasingly prosperous citizens of Yarmouth resenting more and more the arrival of the Portsmen for the herring fair, and their domination of it and of the beach facilities, over which the town had little or no control.

Four years later war with France seemed inevitable, and the Portsmen were called out to carry out a pre-emptive strike, and this they accomplished by destroying the town of Dieppe and attacking French ships assembling in the Seine, thus delaying for months the preparations for the conflict. Later in the same year, in May 1213, a large fleet under the command of William de Longspee, the Admiral who was also for a short time Warden of the Ports, defeated the French in an important naval engagement, the Battle of Damme, the French losing large numbers of ships besides about 200 which were captured by the Cinque Portsmen.

The English fleet included about 50 ships from the Ports, the others being impressed, mostly from the west coast ports.

Two years later, when the quarrel between King John and the barons resulted in the signing of Magna Carta, French invasion preparations were again in hand, and the King spent much of his time travelling between the Ports, on constant lookout for the enemy and encouraging his Portsmen to remain loyal. His misgivings were realised in 1216, when a French invasion force penetrated Kent and achieved considerable success before settling down to lay siege to Dover Castle, the Portsmen meanwhile harrying their supporting shipping with some considerable success.

However, the siege was eventually lifted and a small Cinque Ports fleet, commanded by that gallant old Englishman, Hubert de Burgh, who had just successfully defended the castle against tremendous odds, sailed out from Dover to completely outmanoeuvre and defeat a large French fleet in the Channel.

This encounter, which came to be called the Battle of Sandwich, had important results. It destroyed so much of the French fleet that the threat of another invasion was removed, it ensured enemy inability to renew the threat for several years at least and, most important of all, it introduced a new concept into the Portsmens' fighting technique, since it was the first time they had acted in complete unison as an attacking force manoeuvering so that their total force could be brought to bear on a limited portion of the enemy forces. It was a concept the Portsmen learned well, and is indeed still a classical method and part of naval strategy.

Soon afterwards the Portsmen, essential and admirable as their services continued to prove, were in some disgrace, being summoned to account for their unofficial activities of piracy, robbery on the high seas and pillage. Only Hythe and Rye were apparently blameless. However, the customary exhortation was all that they suffered since, at least for the time, their services to the Crown were so essential that their nefarious activities had to be overlooked.

In the following years they were called out on many occasions, as well as carrying on their own personal war with the people of Bayonne, and frequent rather less violent and bloodthirsty quarrels with the increasingly prosperous and still growing town of Yarmouth.

Piracy reached a new peak in 1235 when the Portsmen were again in disgrace for the seizure and the plundering of French ships when no state of war existed between the two countries, the French ships' letters of safe conduct being destroyed and the crews thrown overboard to drown.

In 1242 Henry III conducted an unsuccessful expedition into France and, smarting from its abject failure, he ordered the Portsmen to harass the coast of Normandy and of Brittany and Boulogne. Only the churches were to be spared. The Portsmen needed no further encouragement and proceeded to create dreadful havoc, until the inevitable happened, and all the French coastal towns, now temporarily at least united in desperation, combined to confront and defeat their tormenters so completely that the Portsmen were bottled up in their home ports, and it was not until the Anglo-French truce of 1243 that they could emerge and resume their more peaceful activities.

In the middle of the century, in the struggles between the King's faction and his opponents, the Portsmen supported first one side and then the other, eventually adding their weight to Simon de Montfort in the Barons' War of 1258-65, and 28 Portsmen served in Simon de Montfort's famous Parliament.

He was appreciative of their support and, in 1264, the Portsmens' ships being worn out from much work and conflict, Simon levied a tax of one tenth upon the clergy, the proceeds from which were handed over to the Portsmen to finance the building of new ships with which to continue their patrolling of the Straits.

In 1277 the King tried to settle the Yarmouth problem. He ruled that the ancient rights of the Portsmen should be respected and that their long enjoyed privileges with regard to the organisation and the control of the great Yarmouth herring fair should continue to be respected, but that the men of Yarmouth should be put in a state of equality with them. It was a settlement acceptable to neither and the quarrel, renewed annually at the fair, and whenever ships of the opposing factions met at sea, persisted until past the middle of the 17th century. If only there had been the foresight and courage to grant Yarmouth a charter, making them a head port of the Cinque Ports federation, much later disagreement and bitter conflict could have been avoided.

Continued patrolling and engagements in the Channel, and in addition the Portsmens' support for Edward I's great Welsh campaign, emphasised their importance to the King and the defence of his realm, so much so that in 1278 he granted the first great comprehensive charter to the ports as a whole, confirming all their ancient rights and privileges, previous ones having in the main been granted to individual towns.

Again in 1282 the Cinque Ports justified their charter, sailing to support King Edward on another Welsh campaign, and in their capture of Anglesea they suffered heavy losses both in ships and in men. In 1290 the King again demanded their service for a major campaign, this time for the conquest of Scotland, a difficult task, since Norman ships were becoming increasingly active, especially in interfering with the ships of the Passage, the Passage still being maintained even when the Cinque Ports contingent was serving the King far away. There were also raids and threats to the ports themselves, besides accelerated losses of their ships during fishing and commercial voyages.

The tension having built up on both sides, the matter came to a head in 1293 when, in defiance of the King, the sailors of the rival nations met for combat at a mutually agreed position. Supporting the Portsmen were Irish, Dutch and Gascon ships, while the Normans enlisted the assistance of the Genoese and the Flemish. This, the Battle of Mahe, resulted in a complete victory for the Portsmen and their allies, though the King was extremely angry at the completely unauthorised combat.

It was the start of a century and a half of war with France and King Edward, realising that somehow the Portsmen had to be controlled, without creating enmity, decided to appoint an overall captain of the Ports, choosing William de Leybourne in 1294.

Soon after, for the first time, an admiral of the Ports was appointed and, though the records are a little unclear, it seems that the first man to serve in this capacity was Gervaise Alard of Winchelsea, who was styled as 'Captain and admiral of the Cinque Ports fleet'. However, since Alard was himself a prominent Portsman engaged in the same heroic services to the King, and the same questionable activities as other Portsmen, the appointment had the rather limited immediate impact that one would expect. The Alard family were an important factor in the life of Winchelsea, and of the ports, for many years. Several of the family are commemorated in fine wall tombs in the north wall of Winchelsea church, and descendants gave distinguished service to the King and the Ports for many years.

In spite of all efforts, the quarrel with the men of Yarmouth continued and, in 1297, when the King in person was in charge of another French campaign, and his invading force of ships had arrived in Swyn, a terrible carnage of the Yarmouth crews took place, the Portsmen burning some twenty of their ships and slaughtering many of their crews, the King himself standing powerless to intervene. In subsequent musterings of large fleets the Yarmouth and Cinque Port ships were kept well apart from each other. This was ensured when both were again mustered at the end of the century for the Scots campaign.

The 13th century was also eventful for other reasons not concerned with war, piracy or robbery on the high seas. The Portsmen continued to work the Passage, carrying Kings and their officers and men, prelates, great officers of church and state, businessmen, and pilgrims across the Straits, handling also quantities of import and export goods and considerable quantities of fish, which they landed and dried on their beaches, and also at the great Yarmouth Herring Fair each autumn.

It is recorded that the barons of the Ports were in London in 1236, to carry the purple silk canopies over Henry III and his queen Eleanor, at their coronation.

Several of the towns had harbour trouble, and worse. Old Winchelsea, which then stood where Camber Sands is now washed by the tides, became steadily less and less habitable, being almost completely inundated by the sea on a number of occasions, particularly in the years 1236, 1250, 1252, and 1254, and at each flooding more and more of the shingle spit on which the town was built was washed away, especially when south-east gales coincided with the spring tides.

Eventually, a particularly severely storm in 1287 resulted in so much damage that it was obvious that the town was becoming unfit for habitation, being an island at each high tide, its houses, its wharves and indeed its whole future in grave danger of being lost completely. It was a disaster for the population, which had built up a considerable fishing fleet and had strong commercial dealings with the continent, especially in the importing of wine, in which it specialised.

Besides this, it had grown to be one of the strongest of the ports, in shipping, in commerce and in manpower. And all this was now at mortal risk.

King Edward I had himself taken great interest in the problem and he decided that, the old town now being untenable, it should be abandoned and that a new town should be built on a hilltop at Iham. It was a remarkable and early example of a carefully planned and regularly laid out town with, at its centre, space for a large and splendid church. The new Winchelsea was finally occupied in 1292, three years after it, and its near neighbour Rye, had received their charters of incorporation, the King having in 1247 taken back into his own hands the rights previously held by the Abbey of Fecamp, thereby freeing them from the domination of a foreign religious institution.

A similar course of action was taken by Edward I in 1290 when Christ Church, Canterbury surrendered most of its hold over Sandwich.

The sea which had so devastated old Winchelsea was already having the opposite effect at Hythe, where the harbour was silting up in the 1203s, and a quarter of a century later Romney was suffering in the same way.

The century ended as it had begun and continued, with violence on the channel coasts, piracy rife, official and unofficial warlike encounters at sea, the continuance though often interrupted of commercial activities, the import and export of goods fraught with continued difficulties, and another Royal charter to the Five Ports and the two Ancient Towns, before the Portsmen yet again put to sea to support another Royal campaign against the Scots.

The 14th century began as the 13th had ended, with constant demands by Edward II for the ship service of the Ports, almost yearly for extended service to support campaigns in Scotland, and in another flare-up in the disagreement with Yarmouth, brought on largely by Yarmouth's increasing irritation with the yearly invasion for the herring fair.

The town, now of course with its own Royal charter, was increasing rapidly in size, prosperity and political and commercial importance, in fishing and in being in a prime situation to act as a major port for the prosperous East Anglian and East Midland areas. Its ample harbour facilities, and its rapidly increasing commercial fleet contrasted strangely with the diminishing facilities of the Ports. Its commercial activities were expanding and its ship service to the King, carried out by the impressment of vessels when they were required, were minimal compared with those born by the Ports.

The Portsmens' less desirable activities continued and a commission to investigate the Portsmens' acts of piracy against the ships and cargoes of the merchants of Flanders in 1310 did little to stem such activity. The King still had urgent need of their services, and the same peacetime vices were of essential value to the King in war.

The incompetent handling by Edward II of the campaigns to Scotland, during which the Portsmen served months over their chartered committment, and without financial compensation, resulted in their increasing reluctance to continue their service, and the King was forced to blandishment and to overlooking their many adventures in order to retain their essential support.

In 1323, when the Scottish campaigns ended, the King of France seized the opportunity to join with the Scots, and by so doing upset the whole precarious balance of power which at that time existed in southern waters, a situation complicated by dynastic problems and uncertainties at home.

The Portsmen who had carried the King and his court to France in great state in 1308 to marry the French princess Isabella, performed their personal service to the Royal house again, by carrying the Queen, her son, and her retinue to the continent in 1325, but little did they know that it would eventually result in the invasion of Suffolk by Mortimer, acting in collusion with the Queen, and the forcible abdication and subsequent murder of the King in 1327. Still less could they have known that the accession to the throne of Edward III would initiate a long reign, which was eventually to prove the beginning of the end of their dominant position in national maritime defence.

There was also an enormous improvement in French naval affairs, in the quality of their ships and crews and in their morale. In consequence French mariners, reinforced by allies, began to take increasing control at sea. The Portsmen alone could no longer withstand the cream of Europe, and so Kings had to muster large fleets, by impressment and other means, from southern and eastern ports.

The balance too had changed, and now the small ships of the Ports were joined by numerous larger ships. In future, except for the more modest engagements, the Cinque Port ships were to be but a modest, and indeed a decreasing, part of Royal fleets.

From 1337 to 1339 the French were in the ascendant, and raided many towns on the coast, including the Cinque Port towns of Hastings, Rye, Folkestone, Winchelsea and Dover, and a little later a squadron of French ships destroyed every single ship in Romney and Hythe.

However the Portsmen, quite accustomed to being in a considerable minority and used to engaging far larger forces than their own, fought back, assembling a small fleet of 21 small ships, augmented by nine others from the Thames, put to sea in 1340, beat off a French squadron attacking Hastings and Rye, and chased them into Boulogne, doing considerable damage to the ships and the town before the arrival of the

King's ships. These and a further 70 ships impressed from the western ports joined the Portsmen in a great sea battle lasting a full twelve hours. They completely destroyed the main French fleet in the Battle of Sluys.

But it was the beginning of the end for the old style of warfare at sea. Marauding expeditions largely gave way to formal battles in which large fleets took part. Individual feats of bravery had to be discouraged in favour of fleet discipline, and larger ships with larger crews were increasingly the order of the day.

It will be obvious therefore that the small Cinque Port ships with only twenty or twenty one men, with limited range in their small open craft, and with a limited number of days of compulsory service per year, were at a great disadvantage, and never again were they to be anything more than a smaller component of a larger force. For instance, when the English fleet of some 700 ships took part in the siege of Calais in 1347, less than a quarter of them came from the Ports, whose ships were henceforth to be of more value in small scale punitive raids, or the repelling of pirates or other raiding parties.

Of the effects of the Black Death in 1348-9 there is little evidence, but the fact that French ships raided Cinque Port harbours seems to suggest that the Portsmen suffered more from the plague than their enemies.

However, English ships, including a large contingent from the Ports, won a convincing victory off Winchelsea in the Battle of Lespagnols Sur Mer. At this time, too, rules were laid down with regard to the necessity of obeying the admiral. His ship was to be the flagship, and be the first to hoist sail or cast anchor. All the ships were to keep in station close to his, and were not allowed to enter a port, disembark crew, or engage an enemy without the admiral's order. It can readily be seen that this was a whole world away from earlier Portsmens' independent behaviour.

The following years were times of hit-and-run raids on both sides of the Channel with sometimes one side, and sometimes the other, in temporary ascendancy, but as has been mentioned, no large-scale fleet sea battles. Seaford suffered a bad French raid in 1356 and Winchelsea, now prosperous and important, suffered again. In fact, during these difficult years the town was raided and sacked no less than seven times.

In that century, too, nature dealt severe blows to the ports. Hastings was a victim of coast erosion, while New Winchelsea, Romney and Hythe were all faced with the constant problem of harbours repeatedly choked with tide-borne shingle. Dover's harbour was also in need of repeated efforts by the townsfolk to keep it clear. In the 1360s, after several disastrous storms, most of Stonar was finally swept away and Sandwich, still with its fine haven, became even more important when the wool staple, which had previously been held by Queenborough, was transferred to it.

The 14th century was a time of town-wall building, and many of the Ports were busy constructing them, since it was realised that it would never be possible to eliminate hit-and-run raids completely. They were not intended to provide defence against a full scale assault, but they could at least delay it until the defences were mobilised.

The last years of Edward III's reign saw a considerable decline of the country's naval power and French raids became more frequent and severe. The portsmen, unable to prevent them, or to destroy the French shipping as once they could, still raised ships and men enough to retaliate on continental ports, so no final advantage was gained by either side. On the other hand piracy and robbery at sea became less common, resulting in the further impoverishment of the Ports. However, in 1394 enough shipping was mustered among them to transport the King and his men to Ireland, and two years later to Calais.

Such activities, some retaliatory raiding on foreign ports, and from time to time warlike activities as part of larger contingents composed of the King's fleet reinforced by ships impressed from western and eastern ports continued, but, as M. Oppenhiem summed up:

'the close of the Fourteenth century saw also the close, practically, of the Cinque Ports era; Winchelsea, Rye, and Hastings were in decadence not only on account of the losses suffered through French attacks, but also from the deterioration of their harbours; the latter cause was also acting at Hythe and Romney, and probably also at Sandwich and Dover, Hythe was afflicted by fire, pestilence, and misfortune of shipwreck. Folkestone harbour was closed in the 16th century, and Sandwich's fine harbour failed when the Wantsum Channel was closed in the same century'.

But although their greatest days had now passed, life in the Ports continued. Fishing, when the harbours silted, was carried on from craft launched from the open beaches, as is still done, for instance, at Hythe and Deal. The great traditional annual expedition to the Yarmouth Herring Fair was still to occur for some time to come, as was the centuries' old feud.

From time to time, in great emergencies, or when some compelling leader arose, flurries of action were once more indulged in. Such a man, for instance, was Henry Pay of Faversham, who captained the Cinque Port ships which were part of the King's navy when it sailed to assist in the crushing of the Welsh rebellion in 1405, and a little later they captured some 120 French vessels and their cargoes of wine, salt and iron.

It is perhaps no coincidence that Henry Pay's Faversham was by this time progressively freeing itself from the trammels of the mediaeval church, in the shape of the Abbot of Faversham Abbey, and therefore growing both in size and in commercial prosperity, situated as it was on a creek, which gave its ships access to the Thames Estuary.

27

Dover, too, in spite of harbour problems, so that much of its shipping had to operate at times from the open beach, continued as did Sandwich in the cross channel ferry services, and some piracy continued, though on a much smaller scale than in earlier times. This change was partly because of Henry V's determined opposition. He had been Lord Warden when his father was King, and therefore had first-hand knowledge. Accordingly he passed an act making piracy high treason. In addition, though he called the Portsmen out for the defence of Calais in 1416, and for the safeguarding of the passage and guarding of him and his entourage and army when they crossed the Channel, he decided to establish his own navy on a larger and more permanent basis, though this policy was not sustained.

By the middle of the 15th century England had largely lost control of the narrow seas and one result was the sacking of Sandwich in 1457. The town recovered slowly and the harbour, though it was beginning to silt, was the assembly point for a large fleet to carry the King and his army to Calais in 1475.

Cinque Ports ships assisted in the carrying of Henry VII and his army to France in 1491 and brought them back, in their role, not as an e´ lite fighting force, but as a transporting group. They performed a similar service for Henry VIII in 1513, for a campaign notable for his victory at the Battle of the Spurs.

A Court of Brotherhood which was summoned at Romney in May of that year ensured that the Portsmen were suitably dressed for that occasion, since it was decided that:

'Every man that goeth in the navy of the Portes shal have a cote of white cotyn with a red cross and the armes of the Portes undernethe that is to say the halfe lyon and the halfe shippe'.

A token force of Cinque Ports ships was present at Dover at the great gathering of ships to take Henry VIII across the Channel for his meeting with Francis I of France. There is some doubt about who was Lord Warden at the time, but it seems that Sir Edward Guldeford, whose appointment was officially stated to be 1521, was in fact acting as Warden. He it was who, because of his Cinque Port status, and as Marshal of Calais, was responsible for providing sustenance for the Royal party for one month. The details were recorded:

'700 quarters of wine, 150 tuns of French and Gascon wine, six butts of sweet wine, 560 tuns of beer, 340 beeves at forty shillings, 4200 muttons at five shillings, 800 veals at five shillings, eighty hogsheads of grease, salt and fresh fish £300, spices £440, diapers £300, 4000 pounds of wax white lights £26 13s 4d, poultry £1300, pewter vessels £300, pans and spits £200, 5600 quarters of coal, tallwood and billets £200, sables £200'.

Sir Edward, on finally achieving his official appointment patent in 1521, was ordered to make similar provision the following year for the visit to Dover Castle of the Emperor Charles V.

After the middle of the 16th century unsuccessful efforts were made to build a new harbour at Hastings, a project which would have been of enormous importance to the town, but the partly completed works were destroyed in a storm which coincided with a high spring tide in 1597. Sandwich harbour, too, which had been failing for years, was the subject of a report in 1574, which stated that it was progressively blocked by sea sand, the flushing action of the waters diminished by the straightening of the river, and by the Abbot of St Augustine's in Canterbury in inning, or draining, the marshes upstream. The result was that the abbot secured more fertile land, and Sandwich lost its haven.

The last offensive operation carried out by the Cinque Ports was in 1588, in England's successful action against the Spanish armada. Exact details of the composition of Portsmens' contribution to the English fleet vary from account to account. However there seems to be a reasonable agreement to the following list: the *Anne Bonaventure* of 70 tons with a crew of 49, together with 11 small vessels (probably fishing boats) as tenders from Hastings, the *Reuben* of 110 tons from Sandwich, and the *Elizabeth* of 120 tons and with a crew of 70 from Dover. Faversham, Hythe, Romney and Rye each sent a pinnace. This is probably not a complete list. In addition five fire ships were prepared at Dover but were not used. They were under the command of the admiral, Lord Henry Seymour.

The great Yarmouth Herring Fair was finally abandoned by the Ports in 1663, when the Ports bailiffs made their final appearance there. The banner they carried for the last time was made in 1632 and now hangs in the council chamber at the Maison Dieu in Dover.

Hastings fishermen and their boats. A mid-19th century drawing.

LEFT: The ruins of the old castle at Hastings. RIGHT: Bulverhythe. The ruins of St Mary, the parish church, all that is left of the old village to the west of Hastings. It once possessed a good harbour. CENTRE: The parish church at Bekesbourne, mostly of Norman origin, but with gothic window insertions, and some 19th century 'restoration'. BELOW: The old Archbishops' Palace at Bekesbourne.

THE HYDNEYE

ABOVE: The Grange or Grench still preserves the ruins of the old prison, and the chapel which is shown here. CENTRE: Hidney, which was always a small village, has been swallowed up by Eastbourne, its old site now occupied by a housing estate and commercial development. BELOW: A fine old 19th century drawing of Pevensey.

ABOVE: The Elizabethan gun, on a modern carriage, preserved in the grounds of Pevensey castle. LEFT: Pevensey courthouse, with the cells and gaolor's room on the ground floor. RIGHT: Pevensey's old mint, now an antique shop. BELOW: Pevensey parish church, now much restored.

ABOVE: The remains of extensive defensive works on the cliffs at the east end of Seaford's sea front. BELOW: Old Rye from the harbour. The church always occupied the top of the hill and was both landmark and outlook.

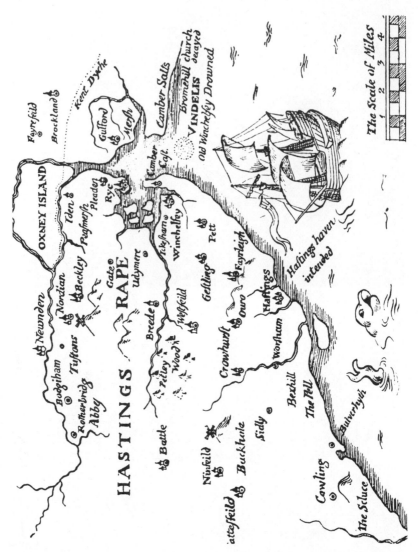

The Scale of Miles

ABOVE: Part of an old map of Sussex by John Norden, added to by John Speed. This shows the coast at the end of the 16th century. OPPOSITE ABOVE LEFT: An old drawing of the Ypres Tower, Rye. RIGHT: The Ypres Tower, now a museum. CENTRE LEFT: The Land Gate in Rye's 14th century town wall, much of which survives. RIGHT: Below the Cupola of Rye's town hall is a carved stone representation of the Cinque Port arms. Now it is sadly weatherbeaten. BELOW LEFT: The clock and quarterboys on Rye church tower. These are replacements for the originals which are still preserved inside the church. RIGHT: The old 15th century Woolpack, next door to the fine town hall of Tenterden.

34

The 19th century interior of Rye parish church. It is
now much altered.

ABOVE: Some of Tenterden's fine old houses
converted for modern purposes. BELOW: Tenterden
from its church tower.

ABOVE: A 19th century drawing of the main street of Tenterden. BELOW: Old houses which once stood in front of Tenterden church. OPPOSITE ABOVE: The old timber house at Smallhythe, next to the church. LEFT: Smallhythe church, a 16th century brick building erected as a chapel to Tenterden. RIGHT: An old drawing of Winchelsea's Strand Gate. BELOW: Winchelsea from the marshes. A 19th century drawing.

ABOVE: A 19th century drawing of the remains of
Winchelsea's chapel of the Grey Friars. BELOW:
Winchelsea in the mid-19th century. This was part of
the 'new town' built on high ground at Iham after the
old town fell victim to storm and sea in the 13th
century.

40

ABOVE: Winchelsea church of St Thomas. LEFT:
The top of the church's entrance porch, showing a
shield bearing the Cinque Port arms. RIGHT: One of
the three fine Alard tombs in Winchelsea church. This
one is thought to be that of Stephen Alard, once
Admiral of the Cinque Ports.

41

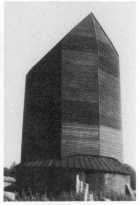

ABOVE LEFT: Winchelsea's old court hall, the upper part of which is now an excellent museum of local history. RIGHT: The old windmill at Iham. It stands on the foundations of the long-destroyed parish church of St Leonard, of Iham village. BELOW LEFT: New Romney's fine 12th century Norman church tower. RIGHT: Old Romney church contains work of many centuries from the 12th century onwards.

ABOVE: The ruins of New Romney's old priory, though how much of it is original is not certain. BELOW: Old Romney church interior. Note the Norman chancel arch, the fine Royal arms and the squints.

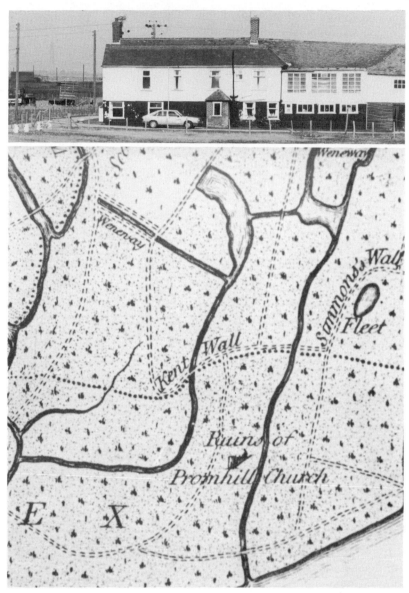

OPPOSITE ABOVE: A view over the town of Lydd, from the church tower.
CENTRE: Lydd from a postcard dated 1906. BELOW: Dengeness and
Oswardstone. A view over the area from the top of the old Dungeness
lighthouse. Somewhere in the middle of the picture was, probably, the tiny
scattered community of Oswardstone. ABOVE: Broomhill Farm, which
perpetuates the old name of Broomhill village, now disappeared. BELOW: An
old map showing the ruins of old Broomhill church.

45

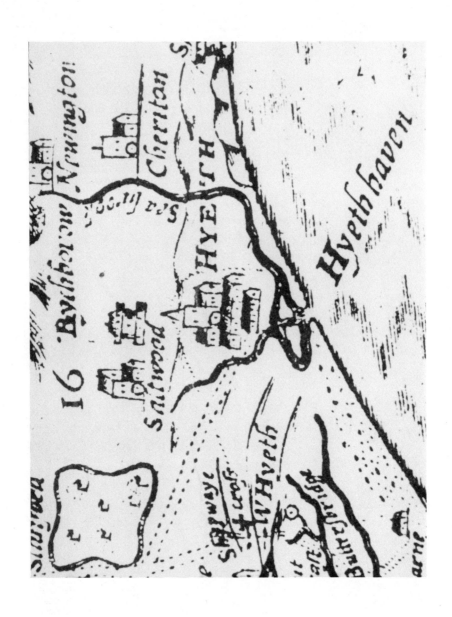

Hythe, shown on Symonson's (16th century) map.
This shows the old Haven, long since silted. Note, on
the left, the original 'Shepways Cross'.

ABOVE: A 19th century drawing showing, left centre, the Army barracks and, centre, the Royal Military Canal. BELOW: Hythe, looking seawards in the 19th century.

ABOVE: Hythe still has its fishing fleet, working now from the open beach. BELOW: The ruins of old West Hythe church.

Manifold Members

Certainly by the 12th century the increase in the services demanded of the ports was too great for the original five to carry it out successfully, and it was necessary to add new members. Two ports, Rye and Winchelsea, at first attached to Hastings, soon became so prosperous and important that they were given head port status, to join the original five. Thus the new title became what it still is: 'The Cinque Ports and the two Antient towns'.

As time went by, other towns and villages were also joined to the federation, some of which eventually became bigger, more prosperous and more important than the particular head port to which they were attached, but none of these were ever permitted to become head ports themselves. They were, and remained 'members' or 'limbs' and were of two kinds; the corporate members which shared most of the privileges and responsibilities with their head ports, and the non-corporate members which had no special privileges but were under the control of their head ports. These enjoyed a somewhat subservient position, but they could look to their head ports for much support and defence against other institutions always ready to impose upon them.

These members, both corporate and non-corporate, joined the federation at different times and for different reasons. Some had little choice, being simply attached to a head port by decree of the Crown, or even in a few cases being simply annexed by a head port. Others sought membership to acquire a powerful ally in times when their already tenuous positions were menaced by great landlords and institutions. Others, such as Brightlingsea, managed to escape from the toils of the mediaeval church, than which there was no harder, or more unscrupulous taskmaster.

Faversham, too, having joined Dover as a corporate member, could summon the support of its head port and the other members of the federation in its continual state of warfare with successive abbots of Faversham, who sought constantly to subdue the town to a state of subservience, a situation of particular offence to the town, which was growing rapidly in power, prosperity and civic awareness and pride.

In many cases the formalities of membership were preceded by unofficial contacts and cooperation, and any date actually given for joining the federation was often little more than the date when formal recognition was given to a union which had already been consummated, and in any case the earliest charters we have for some members may well have been granted years after their original entry.

Certainly, Folkestone joined Dover in the first half of the 12th century and a few years later, Faversham followed suit, while in the mid-12th century Lydd became a member of Romney.

By 1229 Seaford and Bulverhythe certainly had joined Hastings, and Margate came under Dover's wing, while in 1236 Grenche, the modern Grange at the east end of Gillingham, became a limb of Hastings. In the second half of the 13th century Birchington joined Dover, and probably at the same time Stonar linked with Sandwich.

Ramsgate and Walmer were mentioned in Cinque Port documents in 1353 as non-corporate members of Sandwich, but they probably joined Sandwich some years before. Certainly Brightlingsea also joined Sandwich in the second half of the same 14th century, somehow managing to escape from the toils of the abbot of St John's, Colchester.

In the Charter of Edward I to the Ports in 1278 the state of the various ports is given as: Hastings, with Pevensey, Bulverhythe, Petit Iham, Bekesbourne and Grange; Rye; Winchelsea; Romney with Old Romney and Lydd; Hythe; Dover with Folkestone and Faversham; and Sandwich with Stonar, Fordwich, Deal and Sarre.

A complete list of the members was given in the charter of Charles II dated 1688, and quoted by Samuel Jeake in 1728 in his 'Charters of the Cinque Ports, Two Antient Towns and the members'.

In this charter Hastings was recorded as having the two corporate members of Pevensey and Seaford, and five non-corporate: Bulverhythe, Petit Iham, Hidney, Bekesbourne, and Grenche or Grange. Of these Bulverhythe has now been absorbed into the suburbs of its head port, Petit Iham is now a tiny community with the stump of a windmill on the outskirts of Winchelsea, Hidney forms part of Eastbourne, being partly new development and partly industrial estate, Bekesbourne remains an attractive small village near Canterbury, and Grange is now part of Gillingham, Kent.

New Romney had one corporate member, Lydd, which was to surpass it in size and importance, and the non-corporate members of Broomhill, Old Romney, Dengeness and Orwelstone or Oswardstone (there are several different ways of spelling the name of this place).

Broomhill has all but disappeared, its ancient village and mediaeval church gone and the name itself perpetuated in the name of a farm. Old Romney is a small Romney Marsh community with a notable old church, and Dengemarsh is a large tract of land between Lydd and Dungeness with, at its SW corner, an old and a new lighthouse and the great atomic power station of Dungeness. Over Orwelstone or Oswardstone there is a question mark. It seems to have probably been an area of the Dengemarsh, probably a little district with only a few scattered homesteads.

Hythe had no corporate member and only one non-corporate, West Hythe, which now is but a hamlet with a few houses, and a ruined church, only the four walls of which survive.

Dover was well supported. Its two corporate members, Faversham and Folkestone, both became towns of major importance. Faversham prospered early and this prosperity increased when the dissolution of the monasteries in the 1530s freed it from its remaining trammels under Faversham Abbey, with which it had had an increasingly serious number of contentions, and Folkestone, still with its ancient fishing industry, flourished much later, especially as a late 18th century and a 19th century and 20th century holiday town. Dover's non-corporate members were Margate, St John's, Goresend, Birchington Wood alias Woodchurch, St Peter's, Kingsdown, and Ringwould.

Of these Margate has grown to considerable proportions, absorbing St John's into its suburbs. Birchington Wood alias Woodchurch is now a large farming hamlet, Goresend is now represented by modern Birchington, and St Peter's is a community still recognisably a separate area in the now much-developed north of Thanet. Kingsdown has grown somewhat because of its beach, attractive alike to holidaymakers and fishermen, and Ringwould, not having been subject to any severe growth problems, is still a most attractive village.

Sandwich had one corporate member originally, Fordwich, once important as the port for Canterbury. Now a quite delightful sleepy riverside village, it is difficult to realise that, beside its slow running river, there were busy wharves where, among many other commodities, much of the stone for Canterbury Cathedral was unloaded from little ships. Sandwich's non-corporate members were Deal, Walmer, Ramsgate, Stonar, Sarre, and Brightlingsea.

Of these, Stonar disappeared completely, the victim of French raids and storms, its site now developed as a modern factory area. Sarre, now completely landlocked since the Wantsum Channel dried out, is a small hamlet with its memories of its onetime wharves, ferry and windmill. Brightlingsea, a charming yachting and holiday town in Essex, has remained small enough to retain its personal touch and feel and, though its official connection with Sandwich died centuries ago, it has since renewed its links with its former head port and now delights to celebrate its adventurous past as a member of the confederation.

Deal and Walmer, now linked for administrative purposes, were notable for their vulnerability to the threat of offensive seaborne invasions, and their great castles built by Henry VIII. The Goodwin Sands to seaward provided a sheltered area known as the Downs, which offered, and indeed still offers, shelter to shipping in time of storm. Deal in particular profited from the provision of stormbound ships and from pilotage, salvage and fishing. It is now a quietly prosperous seaside resort. Like Ramsgate, Deal has also outgrown its old head port, both securing their own charters, Deal in 1699 and Ramsgate, now a popular holiday resort, in 1884.

The Local Government Acts of the 19th century and 20th century have altered the whole shape of the old federation and removed the last remnants of its former administrative powers, but it still survives as a unique and indeed memorable example of the country's old traditions and history.

The present membership consists of the head ports of Hastings, New Romney, Hythe, Dover and Sandwich, the two 'antient' towns of Winchelsea and Rye, and the members: Deal, Faversham, Folkestone, Lydd, Margate, Ramsgate and Tenterden.

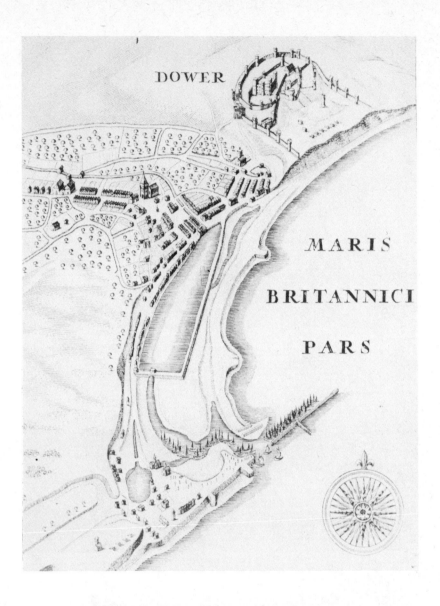

DOWER

MARIS

BRITANNICI

PARS

OPPOSITE ABOVE: Old Dover from the Western
Heights. BELOW: The forebuilding of Dover Castle
and, to its rear, the late 12th century keep. ABOVE: A
late 16th century map of Dover, showing the town,
castle and harbour at that time.

53

ABOVE: The Roman Pharos and Saxon Church of St Mary in Castro in the grounds of Dover Castle. CENTRE: An old 19th century drawing, looking landwards from the Admiralty Pier. BELOW: Dover's old 'trumpet of the Corporation' of the second half of the 13th century. Most of the town's plate was stolen in the 1970s.

ABOVE: The Faversham Moot Horn. One of the oldest moot horns, possibly of late 13th century date. CENTRE: Faversham's old grammar school, built in 1587. BELOW: An old drawing of Faversham. The church tower is still a landmark for miles around.

ABOVE: Faversham Guildhall and Market Place.
BELOW: Folkestone Castle, an earthen motte and
bailey of the second half of the 11th century, and very
little, if ever, used.

56

ABOVE: Old Folkestone, looking westwards. The
parish church stood bare and solitary, but is now
surrounded by buildings and trees. BELOW: Fishing
vessels on Folkestone beach in the 19th century.

OPPOSITE LEFT: Folkestone's Pent Stream once flowed open through the town. It is now covered. RIGHT: Ringwould church with its lychgate and tower, rebuilt in the 17th century. BELOW: The Guildhall. Folkestone. ABOVE: Kingsdown cottages, now in demand as seaside beach homes. The beach was once used by the Ringwould men for fishing from. BELOW: The old entrance to Margate jetty.

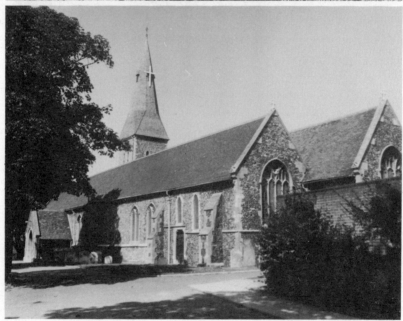

ABOVE: A fine old drawing of Margate Harbour in
the 19th century. BELOW: Once a separate village, St
John's is now swallowed up in Margate.

ABOVE: St Peters still manages to retain its individuality in spite of extensive development. BELOW: The hamlet of Woodchurch, though always small, has almost disappeared. All that remains is a large farm.

ABOVE: The Mayor of Sandwich carries a blackthorn stick. He wears a black robe in mourning for John Drury, the mayor who, with many citizens, was killed in the 1457 French raid on the town. Note that his chain, and the Town Sergeant's hat, carry replicas of the Cinque Port arms. BELOW: Sandwich Quay and the swing bridge, once a toll bridge but now free of toll. The water here, wider in mediaeval times, was the site of the Abbot's ferry.

LEFT: The old Fishergate, which gave access to Sandwich from its riverside wharves. RIGHT: The centre of Fordwich village. The hotel board carries a fine Cinque Port ship as its emblem. BELOW: Fordwich's ancient, and miniature, town hall.

ABOVE: The Rope Walk. The water on the right was Sandwich's 'Town ditch'. BELOW: An early 19th century view of Sir Roger Manwood's grammar school built in 1564. Now known as Manwood Court, it is privately owned.

ABOVE: St Bartholomew's, Sandwich, before it fell into the hands of Sir Gilbert Scott for 'restoration'. It was an early hospice for travellers, and now is sheltered accommodation for elderly residents of the town. BELOW: An earlier bridge over the River Stour, by the town quay.

ABOVE: An early 19th century drawing by Shepherd
of Deal Castle. BELOW: Part of the Barracks complex
at Deal in 1870.

ABOVE: Deal sea front. Note the early bathing 'engine', symbol of Deal's emergence as a seaside holiday town. BELOW: The old church of St. Leonard, Upper Deal. This was the original community of Deal.

ABOVE: An aerial view of Henry VIII's 'great castle of Deale'. LEFT: Walmer Castle, the Lord Warden's official residence, from the gardens. RIGHT: Old St Mary's, the ancient church of Walmer.

ABOVE: Walls of Walmer's ancient 12th century
fortified manor house. BELOW: The old quay at
Ramsgate in sailing ship days.

ABOVE: Sarre, now only a hamlet but once the site of an important ferry, is now noted for its famous old Brandy House. BELOW: The great Georgian house at Stonar still survives, though now shorn of all its former elegant surroundings.

ABOVE: Brightlingsea is still, as it always has been, very much a town of boats and ships, many of which are still built in the shipyards here. BELOW: The beautiful Jacobe's Hall at Brightlingsea is claimed to be one of the oldest inhabited houses in the country. It is said to have been built in 1236 as a moot hall, though it has since been enlarged and much altered.

ABOVE: Here at Reculver, set within the perimeter walls of a Roman fort, are the ruins of two old churches, one Saxon and the other mediaeval. Reculver is listed as being connected with the Ports by some authorities, but not by others. BELOW: Reculver churches from the towers. The foundations of the early Saxon building are shown at the centre foreground.

Privileges

The list of the privileges of the Ports reads like some fine old mediaeval proclamation:

'Exemption from Tax and Tallage, Sac and Soc, Toll and Team, Blodwit, Fledwit, Pillory and Tumbrill, Infrangentheof, Outfrangeneof, Mundbryce, Waifs and Strays, Right to Flotsam, Jetsam or Legan, Privilege of Assembly as a guild, Rights of Den and Strond, and Honours at Court'.

The major rights were supplemented by others of more local importance such as the assize of bread and later supervision of weights and measures.

The exact nature, as well as the spelling, varies a little in differing documents, but the following is a usually accepted list of definitions:

The possession of Sac and Soc gave them full self-government, including the right to organise their own taxation and legal matters.

Toll was the right to levy and receive tolls.

Team gave them authority to compel holders of stolen goods to divulge their source.

Blodwit was the authority to punish shedders of blood, and Fledwit to seize those who fled from justice.

Pillory and Tumbrill, for the punishment of minor misdemeanours; Philipott, in his *Villare Cantianan* notes that 'Tumbrill was an engine much resembling our cucking stool, and was instituted to restrain the fury of loud, clamorous and impetuous women'.

By the possession of Infrangentheof and Outfrangentheof they had the power to detain and execute felons both inside and outside the Ports' own jurisdiction.

Mundbryce was authority to try breaches of the King's peace.

Waifs and Strays conferred the right to take lost or unclaimed goods which had remained unclaimed for a year and a day.

By possessing Flotsam, Jetsam and Legan they had power to claim wreckage when found floating in the sea, cast up on the shore, or goods thrown overboard to lighten a ship in distress.

Being constituted as a Guild gave them authority to 'Act in all causes, including the taxing of all men, for the sake of the common weal', and to gather together at the Court of Shepway 'Where the king's cause could be made known to the Portsmen, and their plaints be respectfully submitted to the king'.

The two quite exceptional rights were Honours at Court: the right to carry a canopy over the King at his coronation and to sit at his right hand side at the top table at the coronation feast, thus giving them immediate access to the King and prominence at a most important occasion, as a mark of their unique importance to the safety of the realm; and Rights of Den and Strond, authority by which they could land on an area of beach at the mouth of the river Yare in Norfolk, now the site of Great Yarmouth, and there mend their nets and set up a fish fair, to which buyers from the prosperous East Midlands and others from Northern Europe, could come and trade for the herring landed in considerable quantities.

It will be obvious that these rights, taken as a whole, quite literally made the Portsmen free men in a basically unfree mediaeval world.

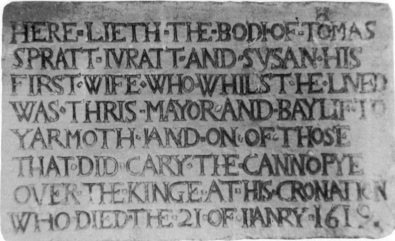

ABOVE: The Barons of the Cinque Ports carrying the canopy over James II at his coronation in 1687. BELOW: The memorial to Thomas Spratt of Hythe, bailiff to the Yarmouth Herring Fair. OPPOSITE: The dress of a Coronation Baron, in the Tenterden museum.

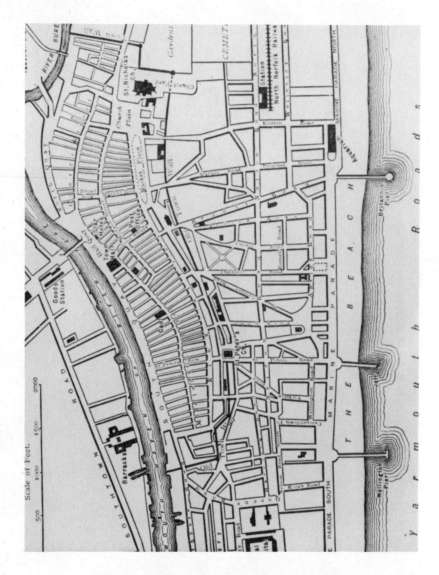

A 19th century map of Great Yarmouth showing the
sandbank built up by the River Yare. The beach at the
bottom of the map was the site of the herring fair.

76

ABOVE: The Parish Church of Great Yarmouth, where services were attended by the Portsmen during the great herring fair. BELOW: The old ice house at Great Yarmouth: evidence of a fishing industry prospering long after the end of the Portsmens' increasingly unwelcome visits.

ABOVE: The ship shown on the Sandwich seal; note the two soldiers in the hull, one carrying a banner and the other a weapon. BELOW: The Dover ship shows two men rowing, one at the steering sweep and masthead castle manned.

78

The Portsmens' Ships

The early Cinque Port ships were small, perhaps of between 20 and 25 tons, open, and in the main propelled by oars, thus accounting for the fairly large crews of 20 or 21 men, a captain and a boy. A single central mast carried a simple square sail of use only when the wind was astern, since tacking in the modern sense of the term would have been impossible. The rudder not having been developed, steering was by a large oar or sweep, worked over the stern quarter of the vessel.

The bows were fine, terminating in an almost knife-edged metal beak, and the whole hull was brought to as smooth a surface as possible, these two attributes making the craft faster and more delicate to handle than those built and used elsewhere, and contributing to the manoeuvre executed so often by the Portsmen in combat with an enemy, of ramming him amidships and cutting him in half.

Such little ships were built on the open beaches in the Ports, the frames produced from trees which had the required curvature in trunks or boughs, and not by sawing to the required shape. These ribs were then planked, the planks not overlapping but butted together, the joints caulked to make them fairly watertight. They were traditional in design and their construction followed well-known methods understood and practised by all. There was no small élite group of specialised craftsmen involved, but it is probable that some men had special skills for the more difficult processes. In the main, the building of these little ships was a communal activity.

The Portsmen used these simple little craft for one of their principal occupations, fishing, and for working the Passage, carrying across the narrow seas Kings, their courts and their armies, diplomats, great officers of church and state, businessmen, traders and pilgrims.

They ventured down the coasts of France and Spain and into the Mediterranean bringing back the wines and the spices from those regions, they sailed northwards and eastwards into the Baltic and they even carried Crusaders to the Holy Land in early days.

They also used them to engage in less desirable activities including piracy, robbery on the high seas, pillaging and sacking continental ports and the ships they found there.

When their ships were required for the King's service they were beached or moored in harbour and large platforms called 'castles' were fitted to bows, stern and masthead. These were called, respectively, the fore castle, the stern castle, and the masthead castle. The fore castle still survives in every ship as the fo'c's'le.

These castles were used for the fighting men in battle, the usual method of engagement being to come alongside an enemy ship, grapple him so that he could not 'escape, so the fighting men in the castles could engage those in the enemy castles until one side or another prevailed. It was really a specialised form of land conflict carried out at sea, archers in the masthead castle using their vantage point to pour arrows into the enemy ranks. The losers, except those who appeared to be suitable for ransom, were thrown overboard to drown, no prisoners being taken. Bearing all this in mind, the Portsmens' preference for ramming and running down the enemy is quite understandable, since it was quick, clean and final.

Most of the towns had seals which incorporated illustrations of such ships, a particularly clear example being that of Sandwich, where the upswept bows and stern, the mast and sail, the steering sweep over the stern, and the three castles are all clearly depicted.

The ship is shown on the sea, in which are swimming five large fish, these two features illustrating two most important occupations of the Portsmen: those of serving the King as his navy, and the more mundane task of fishing.

An 18th century cross-Channel ship being beached at Dover. The similarities between this and early Portsmens' ships are obvious.

ABOVE: The Pevensey seal. The drawing here emphasises the upswept bows and stern and the steering sweep. Here the 'castles' are set well inboard. BELOW: The latest Lord Warden's ship; the Royal Yacht bringing the Lord Warden, HM Queen Elizabeth the Queen Mother to Dover for her Court of Shepway in 1979.

OPPOSITE ABOVE: The Tenterden 15th century ship. Many developments are shown here, including several masts, a stern cabin, and a rudder. From the bow hangs the usual anchor, a fishing net filled with water-worn stones. BELOW: Shipbuilding on Dover beach in the 18th century. This was the traditional method of erecting the frames between vertical posts. ABOVE: This Tenterden seal depicts a late 14th century sailing ship, with the wind astern, a simple rudder, and a large stern castle. BELOW: This Seaford seal shows a fine later mediaeval three masted ship with many details of rigging and cordage.

Mr Ian Gill, LLB, the present Registrar and Seneschal, is the holder of one of the oldest offices, that of being 'the Lord Warden's man', representing him and carrying out his executive functions.

The Lord Warden

The post of Lord Warden evolved during the early years of the Ports from previous attempts to control them and bring them into a unified framework for the defence of the state.

There were, from the 11th century onwards, two fundamental defensive organisations for SE England; the military defensive land position of the great castle of Dover, and the ships of the Cinque Ports, both originally under separate organisation and command. This was a fundamental weakness, since either could deter or inhibit the effective operation of the other.

Sometimes a man of leadership and genius could dominate both. Such a man was the great Hubert de Burgh who, having defended the castle at great odds against the French in 1216, took to the sea in charge of a small Cinque Ports fleet to outwit, outsail and largely destroy the French fleet in the following year.

Thenceforth, the constables or governors of Dover Castle, were also appointed as Lord Wardens. Such men were, William de Averanch, appointed in 1226, and Bertram de Crioll whose formal appointment was either made or his previous appointment confirmed in 1236. He was followed by several others of lesser note, until Richard de Grey, who was appointed Constable of the Castle on 22 June 1258, and Lord Warden on the 23rd. Still the two offices, though now occupied by the same man, were separate appointments.

A noteworthy holder of both was Sir Roger de Leybourne who held them twice, his first brief appointment in 1263; his second, in 1267, lasted until his death 30 years later.

It seems that thenceforth the two offices were not separated, but on the other hand they were never made hereditary, rendering it possible for the King to appoint a strong, able and efficient man, and one perhaps more important, completely loyal.

When a new Lord Warden took office, he assumed a dual responsibility. Appointed by the King, his primary function was to carry the King's commands to the Portsmen and to see that they were carried out. But upon meeting the Portsmen at the Court of Shepway where he took up his office, he also swore to the Portsmen that he would defend and support their chartered rights and liberties. This old procedure is still followed.

Each successive Warden strengthened the office he occupied by every means possible and, from the early part of the 14th century he became, a little at a time, increasingly dominant over the Portsmen, controlling the Court of Shepway, and establishing and developing his courts in Dover to his own advantage and profit.

In return he guarded the Portsmen from many attempts by individuals, and by instruments of church and state, even from county sheriffs and higher courts, to exercise influence over them in defiance of their chartered rights and privileges. They could not be forced to plead in courts, outside the liberties of the Ports, nor in any way to become subject to them.

He claimed the right to enter any of the port towns to do justice there in cases of default and settle any outstanding complaints and quarrels between individuals, or between the ports, which could not be settled in the Portsmens' own organisations, even from time to time using the Portsmens' own courts, such as their Brodhull, if conditions made it desirable and convenient to do so.

He was chief muster master, he appointed inquests into various legal problems and situations, and was a potent force in maintaining the confederation's immunity from the imposition by outside bodies of taxes they were not, by their chartered rights, required to pay. Morover, since his was a Royal appointment, he did not become the member, or the tool, of any one faction, but was responsible for and to them all, and in particular to the King for the performance of the services due to him.

From at least the end of the 12th century the Warden carried out most of the duties which would normally have been performed by an admiral. He held inquests on wrecks, and on ships captured from an enemy, summoned the Portsmen to carry out their chartered duty when they were required, requisitioned additional ships for special purposes, issued licences for the Passage and supervised customs regulations, punished offenders committing offences at sea, and held inquests on bodies washed up from wrecks at sea and headed commissions of oyer and terminer. In addition he took action against organisations or individuals which blocked harbours or navigable waterways.

Many of these duties must have been quite onerous and unattractive were it not that most of the work was done by his staff under the authority of his deputy, and also that considerable profit accrued to the Lord Warden. In particular his share in the salvage of wrecks was considerable.

In the 14th century we find wardens such as William de Clynton, John de Beauchamp and John Beaufort, among others, who also officially held admiral's commands and appointments in the Eastern and Western seas. It is not surprising therefore that by the early part of the 15th century wardens were insisting on the title of admiral, not because of any special appointment, but by virtue of the services they rendered in the ports.

From the beginning of the 16th century the office of Lord Warden became increasingly that of a figurehead, and for that reason and for the social and financial advantages which accrued from the position, it became an increasingly important prize for many in the higher ranks of society. Royal princes and dukes, earls and marquesses all alike held it, and this too was of considerable help to the Portsmen since, although the authority, power and profit of the Lord Warden increased at the same time as theirs diminished, there is little doubt that these distinguished holders brought considerable influence to bear on the appropriate authorities when the power and privileges of the Ports, in later times no longer justified by the limited service they could then offer, were called into question.

One important matter in which the wardens tried to influence the Portsmen quite unduly was in the manner in which they often quite shamelessly tried to force their own nominees on the ports as Parliamentary representatives. The ports were each entitled to nominate two members to Parliament, and these were much coveted by the Lord Warden's friends. At first, one of the two seats was at the warden's disposal and later he even tried, and in some cases actually succeeded in securing both nominations. It was undoubtedly in many cases corrupt, but it was ended by the 1690 statute.

The fact that the office had become one largely of ceremonial was emphasised after the Restoration in 1660 by the appointment to it of James II when he was Prince of Wales. He assumed office at the Bredenstone on Dover's Western Heights in 1668.

In the 18th century Walmer Castle, then a grim decaying 16th century defensive work, was converted into the official residence of the Lord Warden. There is an interesting historical connection here, since this castle was built by Henry VIII in 1539-40. He had served as Lord Warden himself under his father, Henry VII.

During the last two hundred years many famous people have been appointed Lord Warden, among them William Pitt, the Duke of Wellington, Viscount Palmerston, George VI when he was Prince of Wales, Sir Winston Churchill, Sir Robert Menzies (the only Commonwealth statesman to be so honoured) and her Majesty, Queen Elizabeth the Queen Mother.

LEFT: Three vital people at the 1979 Court of Shepway: on the left the Deputy Governor of Dover Castle, in the centre the Registrar and Seneschal and, nearest the camera, the Speaker of the Ports, a post which rotates yearly between the Head Ports. RIGHT: The Silver Oar of Admiralty is carried before the Lord Warden on ceremonial occasions. This example is said to date from the 13th century and to be three feet long, of silver, and with gilt knobs.

ABOVE: The Constable's Tower of Dover Castle. Built in the 13th century after the French siege of the castle had destroyed the old north gate, it is now the residence of the Deputy Governor, a senior Army appointment. BELOW: A modern view of Dover Castle, of which the Lord Warden is Governor.

ABOVE: Dover Castle in the 18th century. This shows the entrance leading to the King's Gate, through which the Lord Warden escorted the King when he stayed in his lodgings here. BELOW: A mid 19th-century drawing of the Lord Warden's flag. It shows the three offices: Governor of Dover Castle, Lord Warden, and Admiral of the Cinque Ports.

The Royal Court of Shepway

The activities of the Portsmen were regulated by courts, the oldest and most important being the Royal Court of Shepway, which was the means whereby the King's commands could be conveyed to the Portsmen through the most senior officer, the Lord Warden of the Cinque Ports. Through him, also, the portsmen could make their representations to the King.

As is the case with most of our ancient institutions, its origins are obscure, but certainly it was in being by 1150, when it was mentioned in an old Hythe charter as if it had already been of long standing.

The court was presided over by the Lord Warden himself, who was always a most senior member of the Royal court, and a man in whom the King could place implicit trust. The post was indeed often held by a member of the Royal family.

Its development proceeded steadily until it reached its real zenith in the 14th century, but from the 15th century much of the detail work with which it had become surrounded was transferred to the Lord Warden's courts at Dover.

The Court of Shepway also came to have important legal functions. Certainly from the end of the 12th century it acted as a shire court where, in particular, crimes against the Crown, such as treason, failure to fulfil or complete the required naval service, counterfeiting the currency and similar matters could be tried. For crimes such as treason there was no appeal from the verdict of the court, the hearing and the sentence being immediately followed by execution, the whole process completed in the single day in which the court sat.

Lesser actions, and in particular appeals from the judgments of the town courts, were also heard and decided.

Disputes between member towns were settled, the guilty town being liable to lose its franchise until the wrong had been corrected.

Though at some periods there were regular once or twice yearly meetings of the court, as its detail work load decreased, much of it transferred to Dover, the assemblies became less frequent.

The representatives of the member towns were always summoned on forty days' notice, much longer than was usual for such events, but necessary when dealing with men who might be away from home for weeks when they were fishing, engaging in commercial activities on the high seas, serving the King, or perhaps engaged in piracy or raids on continental ports. Times when the Portsmen were performing their statutory ship service to the King, or away at the great Yarmouth Herring Fair, were specially avoided.

The court assembled at 9 am, the business arranged by the seneschal, who later became known as the seneschal and registrar, which is still his official title. From the 16th century the principal surviving business was to install a new Lord Warden.

The ancient site of the court is now marked by the Shepway Cross, half a mile to the east of Lympne, Kent. It commands an extensive view over the Romney Marsh, and is situated on a long escarpment which was in fact the clifftop of old England, before the marshes below it were inned and cultivated, thus turning them into enormously fertile land from their previous tidal flats and brackish saltings.

There have been many fanciful suggestions put forward for this choice of position, but the most likely is simply that of geography. In early times roads were but rough tracks and pathways connecting village with village, travel by land was arduous and hazardous, and the Portsmen, who were seafaring men, found it natural to travel on their lawful occasions in their own little ships. A glance at a map will reveal that this site near Lympne was a convenient central place to meet, roughly equidistant from Hastings to the west and Sandwich to the east. Moreover a navigable waterway ran inland from the sea to the foot of the escarpment only a few hundred yards down the hill.

There seems to have been an old stone which marked the site and here, the Right Hon the Earl Beauchamp, KG, the Lord Warden at the time, decided to set up a new memorial cross. When it was completed he summoned a Grand Court of Shepway to meet on 4 August 1923, when it was unveiled and dedicated by the Archbishop of Canterbury. The architect was F.E. Howard and the cross, of Portland stone, was made by the Warham Guild.

This Court of Shepway graced by the Lord Warden, flanked on his right and left by the mayors of the Ports and Antient Towns and their corporate limbs with the maces of their respective boroughs resting on tables in front of them, must have been quite a society occasion, since a contemporary report noted that it was attended also by the Duke and Duchess of Wellington, the Countess Beauchamp, the Earl and Countess Granville, Lord and Lady Northbourne and leaders of local society and other distinguished visitors. These all occupied seats on the dais in front of which were the Coronation Barons. In the main body of the tent was a large gathering of people connected with the Ports 'but of lesser standing'. At the conclusion of the ceremony the deed, by which the Lord Warden conveyed to the corporation of Hythe the land on which the cross stood was sealed by the corporation of Hythe.

There then followed a series of long speeches before the court ended in its usual way, the principal participants being regaled with an enormous meal accompanied by the generous provision of wine.

In fact, however, little use had been made of this site for centuries. Except for one occasion in 1597 when the Court of Shepway was convened at the little village of Bekesbourne, a non-corporate member of Hastings, most were held, at any rate from the end of the 16th century, at Dover, a much more convenient place for assembly, more accessible than the bleak Lympne hilltop. The site chosen was by the Bredenstone on Dover's Western Heights. An early court held here was for the installation of James II.

This 1668 ceremony was described by John Carlisle, Clerk of the Passage of Dover:

'First there came the Guard of Dover Castle, with an horse and pistol each; then Dr. Jenkins, in scarlet, and the judge of the Admiralty Court, in black; the Admiralty Court Sergeant, with silver oar and anchor on it, and the Boder of the castle, with his mace, all bare headed. Colonel John Strode, the Lieutenant of the Castle, came next, and was followed by the Duke of York, accompanied by the Duke of Lenox. After them followed Mr. Jermyn and several persons of quality, succeeded by the five mayors of the ports — Dover, Hastings, Sandwich, Hythe and Romney, and the two mayors of the ancient towns, Rye and Winchelsea, all in black gowns, on horseback, only the mayor of Dover had a white rose. Then seven bailiffs, who are mayors, in their station, in black gowns. Then fortytwo Jurats, who were returned to wait upon the Lord Warden, each attended by a sergeant in livery; then Sir Thomas Armstrong's Troop of Horse, to bring up the rear. There was a sermon preached before the Lord Warden in St. James's Church, and, after the ceremony in the tent, which was erected over the Bredenstone, they all returned to the Castle, where great provision was made, including ten fat bullocks, and a great concourse of people all fed free'.

The ceremonies had by then become little more than a fine spectacle followed by the usual splendid banquet. Indeed, an 18th century wit noted that no such event could be successfully accomplished were it not afterwards consecrated by a generous intake of food washed down with copious draughts of liquor; ale for the common herd, and fine wines for the more delicate palates of the persons of quality who permitted themselves to be present to add an air of respectability to the whole affair!

Certainly, food and drink were not overlooked in the planning of later ceremonies. An account of the dinner given by Lionel, Earl of Dorset and Middlesex on his being appointed Lord Warden by Queen Anne in 1709 details the expenses as follows:

'£214. 10. 3 paid to Mr. Russell, the Dover cook. £76. 16. 9 for the outcharge and expense (butlers, cooks, hire of crockery, coaches, etc.

First course.

5 sorts of Soups, 12 dishes of fish, 8 dishes of pullets, 1 Westphalia ham, 12 haunches of venison, 6 dishes of roast pigs, 3 dishes of roast goose, 12 venison pasties, 12 white fricassees, 8 dishes of veal.

Second course.

14 dishes of ducks, turkeys and pigeons, 12 dishes of roast lobsters, 15 codlin tarts creamed, 14 dishes of humble pies (liver and heart in if of deer), 10 dishes of fried fish, 8 dishes of chickens and rabbits, sweetmeats, jellies, syllabubs and cream, fruit, almond pies etc. On side tables a large chine of beef stuck with flags and banner'.

There was no record of liquid refreshments but they must at least have been reasonably adequate, to judge from the list of breakages which were: 8 dozen glasses. 12 salvers, and 120 jelly glasses.

From the middle of the 19th century, extensive military works and the presence of a large garrison of soldiers rendered the Bredenstone increasingly inconvenient, and a new venue was adopted, in the grounds of Dover College, which had previously been a farm and before that part of the old Dover Priory of St Martin of the New Work. Here, since the end of the 1939-45 war, three specially notable Lord Wardens have appeared at the Court Of Shepway; Sir Winston Churchill the great wartime leader, Sir Robert Menzies who was the first Commonwealth statesman ever to hold office and most important of all, and reverting to many ancient Royal appointments, H M Queen Elizabeth the Queen Mother.

The general order of the ceremony differs little from occasion to occasion, and much of it is of ancient origin. After a religious service, now held in the church of St Mary in Castro in the castle grounds, the new Lord Warden is offered the key of the castle, which is presented on a cushion, and its acceptance is signalled by touch. This is followed by a procession, preceded by a ceremonial guard, of the various dignitaries, consisting of the mayors and representatives of the Ports, the Barons of the Ports, the deputy Constable of Dover Castle, and then the Lord Warden, who is preceded by an official carrying the silver oar, the visible symbol of his authority. Representatives of the government, church, and many distinguished guests are also present.

At the Court of Shepway, now held in a great marquee, the proceedings open with the Proclamation, read by the Seneschal and Registrar:

'All Mayors and Barons of the Five Ports and their members, summoned and warned to appear in their proper persons before my Lord Warden at this the Queen's Majesty's Grand Court of Shepway, here to be holden this day, draw near and give your attendance to the Court, upon the peril that shall fall of it'.

There follows the readings of the Lord Warden's Precept and the returns made to the summons by the members of the Ports, after which the Seneschal announces that the Court is duly formed, and the Lord Warden's patent is read.

The Speaker of the Ports, an office which rotates yearly between the Ports, then addresses the new Warden:

'My Lord Warden, I have the honour to inform you that the Barons of the Cinque Ports have appointed me their representative at this Grand Court of Shepway, and in this capacity it falls on me to request your Lordship to undertake the duties of the ancient and honourable Office of Lord Warden of the Cinque Ports and in the performance of the same to observe and uphold the franchises, liberties, customs and usages of the Ports'.

The Lord Warden's reply is an undertaking to the Ports which is that given to the Portsmen through all the centuries by each new Lord Warden, to maintain all their ancient rights and privileges:

'Mr. Speaker, in response to your request I have great pleasure in assuming the duties of the ancient and honourable Office of Lord Warden of the Cinque Ports, and I undertake in that capacity to maintain the franchises, liberties, customs, and usages of the Ports'.

The customary ceremonial completed, the Seneschal, after a speech by the Lord Warden, announces the closure of the Court:

'All Mayors, Barons, and others that have had to do at this the Queen's Majesty's Grand Court of Shepway, before my Lord Warden this day, shall depart and take your ease unto a new warning. God save the Queen, my Lord Warden, and all the Court'.

The day ends in traditional fashion with a banquet, of more modest proportions than in earlier years when it was once held in the open, or in a tent, at Shepway Cross, and later in Saltwood Castle, but now in the old Maison Dieu, the town hall of Dover. In this fashion the tradition of more than nine eventful centuries is yet preserved and honoured.

A Court of Shepway is incomplete without the Coronation Barons in their distinctive dress. These are life appointments, those so honoured being mayors of the Port towns at the time of a coronation.

In 1902 the *Dover Express* published a detailed description of the dress worn by the Barons in the Court that year:

'A rich silk velvet coat, lined throughout with white silk. Silk velvet breeches. White silk velvet waistcoat, embroidered with flowers of the early Victorian period, lace ruffles and jabot, and velvet cap. The robe — of special design and made of rich scarlet cloth, lined with white silk, and with blue velvet facings, and edged with gold lace. The bars and arms of the Cinque Ports will be embroidered on the right shoulder'.

LEFT: The Shepway Cross, near Lympne. RIGHT: An old view of the interior of St Mary in Castro, where the hallowing service has been held since the 17th century. CENTRE: What remains of the Bredenstone today. BELOW: The third and present venue for the Court of Shepway, in the grounds of Dover College, the Queen Mother arriving for the 1979 Court.

ABOVE: Dover's Bredenstone in the 17th century. The site of the Court of Shepway from the 17th century to the end of the 19th century. BELOW: The banquet at the installation as Lord Warden of Lord Palmerston in 1861.

ABOVE: The Installation as Lord Warden of the
Marquess of Dufferin and Ava in 1892. BELOW: The
1896 Court of Shepway in the grounds of Dover
College for the installation of Lord Salisbury.

ABOVE: Lord Brassey at his Court of Shepway installation in 1908. BELOW: Earl Beauchamp at the Bredenstone. He was Lord Warden from 1913 to 1934.

The procession to the 1923 Court.

ABOVE: The 1923 Court in session . The legal figure, standing, is the Registrar and Seneschal. The Lord Warden's standard forms the backcloth. BELOW: The Marquess of Reading at his Court of Shepway in 1934.

INSTALLATION

OF THE RIGHT HONOURABLE

WINSTON SPENCER CHURCHILL

O.M., C.H., LL.D., Constable of Dover Castle,

as Lord Warden and Admiral of the Cinque Ports,

at a Meeting of the Grand Court of Shepway, at Dover, 14th August, 1946.

OFFICIAL PROGRAMME.

1. The Mayors of the several Corporations, Barons, and all persons who are to take part in the Installation will be at the Keep in the Castle by 10.15 a.m.

2. A Service will be held in the Church of St.-Mary-in-the-Castle at 11 a.m. (His Grace the Lord Archbishop of Canterbury, the Rt. Rev. the Lord Bishop of Dover, Chaplain of the Cinque Ports and the Rev. J. C. Purves, Senior Chaplain of the Forces).

N.B.—Admittance to the Castle will be by tickets issued only to the Members of the Court and those invited by the Lord Warden.

3. The procession will then be formed and proceed from the Constable's Gate down Castle Hill Road, by way of Castle Street, Market Square, Cannon Street, Biggin Street, Priory Street, and Folkestone Road to St. Martin's Priory (Dover College), where the Grand Court of Shepway will be held at 12.15 p.m.

4. After the Ceremony the Luncheon given to the Lord Warden by the Cinque Ports will be held at the Town Hall. Ladies and Gentlemen having Luncheon Tickets should be at the Town Hall by 1.30 p.m.

ORDER OF PROCESSION.

MEMBERS OF COURT OF SHEPWAY.

The Mayors of the Cinque Ports, Ancient Towns and their Limbs, accompanied by their Recorders, Town Clerks, Chaplains and Clerks of the Peace with their Barons or Returned Men, preceded by their respective Mace Bearers and Officers in the following order:—

Ramsgate.
Margate.
Tenterden.
Deal.
Folkestone.
Faversham.
Lydd.
Winchelsea.
Rye.
Hythe.
New Romney.
Dover.
Sandwich.
Hastings.

Barons who attended the Coronation of King Edward VII., King George V., or of King George VI., in their Robes.
The Registrar of the Ports.
The Chaplain of the Ports.

ABOVE: The 1946 Court of Shepway programme, when Sir Winston Churchill was installed as Lord Warden. OPPOSITE LEFT: Sir Winston Churchill in procession at the 1946 Court. RIGHT: The 1946 Court of Shepway procession leaves the Castle. BELOW: Coronation Barons at the 1966 Court.

OPPOSITE ABOVE: Sir Robert Menzies, towards the close of the 1966 Court, reads his speech of acceptance. CENTRE: The 1979 Court of Shepway in progress. BELOW: Cinque Port mayors, barons, and representatives of Church and State at the 1979 Court. ABOVE: The Lord Warden, HM Queen Elizabeth the Queen Mother, pays close attention to the ceremony.

ABOVE: The Dover group, and BELOW: from Deal.

ABOVE: From Faversham, and BELOW: from Tenterden.

Legal, administrative, and religious bodies' representatives. The Registrar and Seneschal is in the centre,
and the Bishop of Dover on the right.

Admiralty, Lodemanage, Brodhull and Guestling

With the growth of the confederation, the old Court of Shepway ceased to be adequate for the increasing administrative and legal processes of the organisation, since it met only occasionally and often irregularly, and for only a single day, all its business having to be completed before sundown. Furthermore, a full forty days' notice had to be given to the various ports before it could sit.

Besides this, the growing power of the Lord Warden gave him the authority to become more active in the Confederation's affairs and, since he was also the governor of Dover Castle where he had his own instrument, often styled 'the Court of the Castle Gate' for the regulation of the affairs of the Castle garrison, it was not surprising that he should attempt to use it also for control over the Ports. This was irregular, since the Castle was outside the jurisdiction of the Ports, being to them 'in the foreign' and therefore its court could not legally be used for the regulation of the Portsmens' affairs, such actions being construed as subverting their privileges granted in many Royal charters.

The matter was a contentious issue for years until, about the middle of the 14th century, some solution had to be found, the Court of Shepway being clearly increasingly inadequate and unsuitable, and the Castle court illegal.

By what means is not known, the Lord Warden set up his court in old St James's Church at the eastern end of the town and immediately below the Castle cliff, and it was held in the south aisle of the nave until the 19th century. Old St James's, being situated close to the old harbour and in the town, was a convenient site readily accessible both by sea and by land.

The Court of Shepway continued to be used for the installation of the Lord Warden and other important Royal occasions to provide a link between sovereign and the Portsmen, as a Court of appeal against judgments given in the various local authorities courts and assemblies, and for the trial of charges of treason, counterfeiting and matters of treasure trove.

Succeeding Wardens developed the court at St James's, and by the end of the 16th century it functioned as a Court of Chancery, and became known by that name, in which state it continued until it was finally discontinued.

The development of this court and its importance to the Cinque Ports is well described by Murray:

'The successive holders of the office of Warden, in fact, evolved out of the old Courts of Shepway and of Dover Castle, held in their capacity as Warden and as Constable respectively, a new court which was much more powerful than either - - - To its success was due the preservation of the immunity of the Ports from the jurisdiction of the courts at Westminster, and so in large measure the survival of the confederation after the collapse of its naval importance.'

The various duties carried out both by and for the Warden included many which were properly his concern as Admiral of the Ports. To carry them out Courts of Admiralty were used, and these were for several centuries held on the beach conveniently near to the place where the incident, such as a wreck or a stranding, took place. Sometimes, when a member was involved, they were held in that member's head port, while those of Dover, and often also of its members, came increasingly to be held at the Warden's Dover Courts.

Here, his courts of Chancery and of Admiralty seem to have worked closely together and their history is now difficult to separate, since some of the proceedings of the Admiralty Court seem to have been recorded in the Chancery Court documents. After all, the same people, using largely the same machinery, were responsible for the operation of both.

In spite of considerable pressure, other Portsmen were stubbornly opposed to coming to Dover to appear at the Admiralty Court, maintaining that the old method of holding court in the various head ports or at another nearby convenient venue should continue, the Court moving from port to port as necessary. However, in the 17th century opposition seems to have been fruitless, and all the Ports were summoned to joint sessions in Dover, until the middle of the 19th century.

From at least the early years of the 16th century, and probably even earlier, many Portsmen were engaged in piloting ships through the always dangerous narrow seas of the Dover Straits to and from the Thames Estuary, the East Coast ports, and those on the other side of the Channel in NW Europe.

The first Court of Lodemanage was set up by the Lord Warden in 1526 to organise and regulate pilotage on a proper basis, the organisation itself being called the Trinity House of the Cinque Ports. However, a few years later the words Trinity House seem to have been discarded and the name 'Cinque Ports Pilots' came into general use.

The controlling Court of Lodemanage admitted only suitable and knowledgeable pilots, who were designated Lodesmen, and regulated their services and the fees they charged.

It also in course of time arranged for the annual sounding of the Channel from the Nore to the South Foreland, and decreed that some pilots should always be in ships at sea, except in severe gales, to be ready to board any ship which required one. Later, lookout points were established, and staffed by pilots who were next in turn to take their period of duty.

Dissenters or other non-churchmen were not allowed to serve as pilots. The pilots themselves built a small gallery at the west end of St Mary the Virgin's church in Dover, access to it being gained, not from the body of the church, but by a ladder from the entrance lobby beneath the western tower. Pilots could therefore always be summoned in time of need, and leave the church, without disturbing divine service. Later, pilots were stationed in other Cinque Port towns and other similar galleries were built in several churches, a notable example being that of St Leonard's, in Upper Deal.

This court was put on a much more formal basis in the reign of William III, so that it was controlled by the Lord Warden, the Lieutenant of Dover Castle, the captains of the three castles in the Downs, Sandown, Deal and Walmer, and the mayors for the time being of Sandwich and of Dover.

It is recorded that the last session of the Court of Lodemanage was presided over in the hall of old St James's Church on 21 October 1851 by the old Duke of Wellington, the Lord Warden, only a few months before he died.

The court was then closed and the pilots came under the Master and Brethren of Trinity House, Deptford.

The Court of Shepway, and the Warden's courts at Dover, being overwhelmingly legalistic in character, did not provide the Portsmen with forums for discussion or the resolution of many internal matters of the Confederation which were important to them and, to fill the need, the Courts of Brotherhood and Guestling evolved internally, growing no doubt originally out of more informal discussions and gatherings. The original name of the Court of Brotherhood was Brodhull.

The Court of Brotherhood was by far the oldest of the two, and the most important. Its membership was confined to nominees of the five ports and two antient towns only. It was mentioned in old records from the 13th century onwards, its origin lying possibly in an even more ancient assembly thought by some to have been held in or near Dymchurch, perhaps in early times connected with the affairs of the Marshmen.

Though the Brodhull was the Portsmens' own organisation, developed by them and used for their own purposes, Kings and wardens certainly did, upon occasion, avail themselves of its services, as was the case for instance in 1224, and again in 1282 and 1297. This was possibly because such a forum was more convenient for the carrying

111

out of special business not normally part of the increasingly formal character of the Shepway procedure, and perhaps also because a Brodhull could be summoned in emergency at only a few days' notice.

The main business of the Brodhull was the preseration and supervision of the Portsmens' chartered rights and interests, and it was divided into three principal matters: 1 The organisation of the appearances at coronations, known as 'Honours at Court'; 2 The arrangements for the conducting of the Yarmouth Herring Fair; 3 The countering of the hostility of people and institutions to the rights and privileges of the Ports, and to the opposition of the whole Confederation to any attempts to limit or deny them.

In the 14th century the Brodhull seems to have been fully developed and the agreement of 1357 laid it down that each of the head ports was to elect from its number jurats to represent them in the Brodhull, the numbers varying from time to time.

Honours at Court arrangements often had to be made at short notice, since often little time elapsed between the death of one King and the coronation of his successor. The honour of carrying a canopy over the King and his queen when they walked in procession on their coronation day, involved each canopy being supported at its four corners by lances, or later, slim poles, carried by the Portsmen who also enjoyed the right to sit on the top table at the King's right hand for the coronation banquet.

At first, one jurat from the Ports was used at each lance, but later several were nominated for each, taking it in turn. These jurats were carefully chosen so that their appearance was a credit to the organisation, and they were all dressed identically, in dramatic and colourful robes, knee breeches and scarlet capes, with brightly decorated waistcoats, and buckled shoes. Their exact function, and their bearing, all had to be carefully rehearsed so as to create the maximum impact.

The arrangements for the Yarmouth Herring Fair were much more prosaic, and involved two Brodhulls, one before and the other after the fair.

At the first, the bailiffs, whose task it would be to control the various events of the fair, gave minute attention to protocol lest the other side should secure an advantage for which they were always seeking and watching. Those selected by each of the head ports from among their own jurats appeared in person before the Brodhull, to be approved by the assembly (and some were not) and were then given firm directions on all aspects of the organisation, though new jurat-bailiffs usually had the support of some at least who had served before.

The second Brodhull, after the Fair, gave detailed consideration to its success or failure, and each of the bailiffs, in turn, gave his verbal report to the members of the Brodhull and was in turn questioned by them. This careful control was to ensure the consideration of their many rights during this event.

The third important part of the Brodhull's work, which developed considerably in the 14th and 15th centuries, was to counter hostility, particularly of the older institutions, to the maintenance and expansion of the federation itself and its chartered rights. Such expansion of course usually involved a similar contraction in the rights of other bodies, and this was particularly resented by the many religious orders of the mediaeval church.

The Abbot of Battle fought a bitter fight with the Portsmen over the loss of his rights and his income accruing from Dengemarsh, when it was joined with Romney as its head port, and the Abbot of St Augustine's in Canterbury reacted similarly when Stonar was prised from his grasp and joined to Sandwich. A later Abbot had his revenge when, by altering the river banks and inning much of the lower marshes of the lower reaches of the River Stour, he lessened the efficiency of the water to scour out accumulations of sand from the haven's mouth. He secured extra valuable cultivated land, and Sandwich lost its haven.

Perhaps the most striking, and indeed the most persistent and bitter, of all these confrontations with the religious houses was that between the town of Faversham and the Abbot of Faversham Abbey. He of course lost much profit and, even worse from his point of view, his control of the town, when Faversham joined the Confederation, and he subjected the townsfolk and especially its civic leaders, to a vitriolic campaign which lasted for many years, and at one time involved the Lord Warden, the Court of Shepway, the King and the Pope. Quarrels and disagreements rumbled on, occasionally flaring up into open confrontation, until at last the dissolution of the monastic houses provided a welcome and final solution.

Brightlingsea, also, managed to prise itself free from the clutches of the Abbot of St John's, Colchester, and the Abbot lost much profit and control of the town, including his right to have, and to use, his own gibbet there.

This part of the Brodhull's work in safeguarding the rights and privileges of the Ports, and also of extending them where possible, was formalised in the 1392 agreement, which also decreed that the costs of this work should be shared by all the members of the court.

From 1433 the White and Black books, which were kept at Romney, recorded the details of these Brodhulls and the meetings of the Court of Guestling. The White Book contains the records from 1433 to 1571 and its successor, the Black Book, those from 1572 to 1955.

The work of the Brodhull gradually diminished, a change hastened by the dissolution of the religious houses, which at a stroke removed

113

one of the Portsmens' principal enemies, and the ending of the Ports' participation in the Yarmouth Herring Fair in the 17th century removed all the administration previously necessary for that.

The Brodhulls have now lost their administrative and other essential functions, and are summoned only occasionally to celebrate special events and for social functions, when they usually share the same time and place with the Court of Guestling.

There were many matters for discussion which affected not only the head ports, but also the members, for which there was no proper machinery. Undoubtedly in early times much was done in this field by informal meetings and assemblies but, when the membership of the Confederation increased, this was not so easily arranged, especially when the head ports needed to consult the members on such things as the allocation of responsibility for ship service, legal matters, debts, internal taxation and expenses.

An assembly of the western ports, Hastings, Rye and Winchelsea, took place in the 14th century and this became known as a Guestling, probably because the little village of Guestling was the site of the meeting. It was in a convenient situation in the hinterland behind the three ports, yet it belonged to neither. It was neutral ground. Its date of founding probably predates this meeting for perhaps as much as two centuries and its survival indicates that its participants must have found it useful.

In the 15th century the eastern ports also seem to have adopted the idea. In 1525, according to the Romney records, Sandwich arranged for a Guestling to be held in Dover. The summons read:

'For asmych as of late date there hath been a Guestling holden at Winchelsey - - - we therefore have devised a gestlyng to be holden in Dovorr'.

At first Guestlings were held in various locations but later, certainly from the early 17th century, they seem to have been combined with the Brodhull, both held at Romney and apparently using the same administrative machinery. Hence in later years we usually hear of a Brodhull (later a Brotherhood) and Guestling.

It appears that the Brodhull House at Romney, apparently in early times both owned and maintained by the Brodhull, was small, since the arrangements were that the Brodhull, consisting only of representatives of the seven head ports, first met in this house, and then joined the representatives of the members in the nave of Romney parish church, where of course there was ample room for all for the Guestling.

114

ABOVE: An early drawing of old St James's. BELOW: This early view of old St James's shows the lean-to extension on the left, which was used for the Warden's courts in Dover.

CINQUE PORTS
Courts of Brotherhood and Guestling

Thursday, 24th Sept., 1953

The Courts will assemble at the Town Hall and proceed in procession to S. Mary's Church, where a Service, which the public may attend, will be held at 11 a.m. Seats must be taken by 10.50 a.m.

The Meeting of the Courts will be held at the Town Hall at 12.15 p.m. A limited number of seats will be available for the public and tickets of admission may be obtained on application at my Office on the 22nd instant.

JAMES A. JOHNSON,
Town Clerk.

Town Clerk's Office,
New Bridge House, Dover.
19th September, 1953.

ABOVE: The ground inside the ruined walls of St James was the floor of the old courtroom. It was entered through the doorway at the centre of the picture. LEFT: The Lord Warden's seat which was originally in the annexe to St James's. It is now in Dover Museum. The Lord Warden or his Deputy sat on the raised seat, flanked on his left and right by his officers. RIGHT: The summons to the court of 1953. Mr James Johnson, who issued this notice, was Registrar and Seneschal of the Confederation for a number of years.

ABOVE: The old parish church at Guestling, probably the original site of the Court of Guestling. BELOW: New Romney (the Cinque Port Romney) was the traditional site, and the place of storage of the records, the White and Black Books in particular, of the Portsmens' own courts.

ABOVE: The meeting of the Courts of Brotherhood
and Guestling in 1902. BELOW: The meeting of the
courts in 1925.

Arms and Seals

Like most institutions, the Cinque Ports possess distinctive heraldic devices and seals, many of which are of early date.

The heraldic device which was common to most, and used also by the Lord Warden himself, and by the bailiffs of the Ports, consisted of the foreparts of three lions joined to the stern halves of three ships or, in heraldic language: 'Three lions passant guardant conjoined to as many ships hulls', a device which has been said to be the most curious frolic in heraldry.

Each town had its own variations. For instance Hastings has a half lion joined to a half ship at top and bottom, the middle figure being a whole lion, while Sandwich's lions are almost whole, only the nearside leg and the root of the tail being omitted.

Dover's ships' sterns are shown only stylistically, Rye's ships are shown at an angle to reveal the elegant curved lines of the hull, and the stern, of course at this early date, rudderless. Winchelsea's ships exhibit rather later sterns incorporating rudders.

A 15th century three-masted ship with a cabin at its stern, and a rudder, and with a large square sail bearing the distinctive three lions and three half ships motif of the Ports on its central mast, forms the arms of Tenterden. Such a ship was apppropriately shown as part of the town's heraldry since Tenterden was incorporated in 1449, its little port of Smallhythe then still working and still building ships.

Of more recent arms, that of Margate carries a single half lion and a half ship, as does Ramsgate. Folkestone similarly has the one motif instead of three, on a shield in the centre of the arms, but this is accompanied by a fine, traditional Cinque Ports ship with its three castles, a furled square sail on its single central mast and a crew of four, all staring earnestly forwards.

Deal's arms, granted in 1968, include a shield with the three half lions and three half ships, surmounted by the silver oar of Admiralty.

The seals of the Ports are of particular interest, since most of them carry a representation of a Cinque Ports ship. Most of the towns in the Confederation either possess, or once possessed, several of different periods, the earliest ones being somewhat crude and simple, but many of the later ones are crisp and full of detail.

119

Early ones are those of Rye, Fordwich, Dover and Faversham, among others, while 13th century examples such as the common seals of Hastings, and of Faversham, Hythe, Pevensey and Dover, are fine illustrations of early Portsmens' ships, perhaps one of the most detailed of the period being that of Sandwich. It depicts one of the Sandwich ships fitted out with its three castles as symbols of the town's naval obligation to the Crown, a symbol accentuated by the two men in the bows, one carrying a battleaxe and the other a banner. The five fish swimming in the sea beneath the ship represent the town's important civil occupation of fishing.

Another fine seal is that of Hythe, which the town uses for many purposes, including decorating the sign boards at the town's entrances, making an unusual and specially apt introduction to this fine old place.

It too uses the symbols of the castles on the ship, and the fish in the sea to signal its principal occupation.

The common seal of Lydd, also used as a town sign, bears on its left side a church with a tower surmounted by a steeple and, on the right, the stern half of a ship with a furled sail on a single central mast. The Lydd bailiff's seal however is curious, since it bears the usual Cinque Ports' motif, but reversed, so that the half lions are to the right and the half ships to the left. This is also used as their arms and in full colour it creates a most pleasing effect.

As might be expected, later seals are fine, with much fuller detail as a general rule. Tenterden's mid-15th century common seal shows a single-masted ship with a square sail carrying the Cinque Ports motif of the half lions and half ships, but perhaps the most detailed is the 1544 common seal of Seaford. This shows, in some detail, a Tudor three-masted ship with a crow's nest on each tapered mast, rope ladders, and details of the rigging.

The Lord Warden's standard bears the Cinque Ports motif, castles, and an anchor surmounted by a coronet.

This symbolises his various offices, his full title being: 'Constable of Dover Castle, Lord Warden and Admiral of the Cinque Ports, two Antient Towns and their members'.

The banner of the Cinque Ports bailiffs. This was
made in 1632 and used each year at the Yarmouth
Herring Fair until the Portsmen attended there for the
last time in 1663. It now hangs in the Maison Dieu,
Dover.

LEFT: The Cinque Ports arms depicted on the town boards of the Ports. RIGHT: The middle figure of the Hastings arms is a complete lion, an interesting variation. BELOW: The Dover arms. The left circle depicts a Cinque Ports ship, while that on the right shows St Martin, the town's patron saint.

122

LEFT: Carried on a shield on the Dover arms, the sterns of the ships are figurative rather than, as is more usual, detailed. RIGHT: The Sandwich arms take several slightly different forms. This example is on the exterior of the Guildhall. BELOW: Rye uses its arms on its town sign. The sterns of the three ships are unusual.

PORTA·MARIS·PORTUS·SALUTIS

SALUS·NAUFRAGIS·SALUS·ÆGRIS

SALUBRITAS ET AMOENITAS

OPPOSITE LEFT: The Tenterden arms, one of the finest of the Ports, shows a mid-15th century ship with the Ports arms carried on a square sail. Note the rudder, the anchor, and the cabin at the stern. RIGHT: The Margate arms granted in 1858. Here a single half lion and half ship is placed above the white horse of Kent. BELOW: The Ramsgate arms. The four quarters of the shield bear representations of the white horse of Kent, the Cinque Ports lion and ship device, a dolphin and an old Cinque Ports ship. ABOVE: Granted in 1958, the Folkestone arms are shown on a shield with two supporters, that on the left representing St Eanswith, and that on the right William Harvey, discoverer of the circulation of the blood in the human body.

125

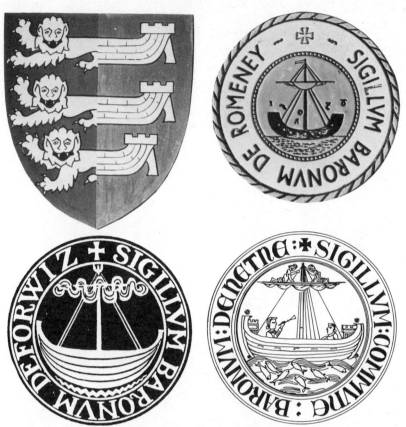

OPPOSITE ABOVE: The Deal arms carries the usual Ports arms upon a shield, but also above them the Lord Warden's Oar of Admiralty. Supporters are a Roman soldier and a Royal Marine. BELOW: Some Ports have no arms, but use variations of their seals, like this of Hythe. It is said that the ship shown with its castles and with a man sounding a trumpet is recognition of Hythe's ship service, and the seven fish refer to the seven head ports and to the town's major fishing industry. The crosses represent the Archbishop's holdings in the area. ABOVE LEFT: Several of the Ports also were content to use variations of the Warden's arms. This is one of several examples used by Winchelsea, carved over the porch of the parish church. RIGHT: Romney uses its old seal as its arms. These are shown on the town hall and upon the town signs. A simple example of a Cinque Ports ship. BELOW LEFT: Fordwich, like Romney, also has a simple old ship for its seal and for its arms. RIGHT: A line drawing of the Hythe seal.

ABOVE: The Lydd common seal, which also serves as
the town's arms. This is a variation of the usual
Portsmens' seals, showing half a ship conjoined with a
church. BELOW: A Winchelsea seal, of which there
are several variations.

ABOVE: A Rye seal. BELOW: A Pevensey seal.

ABOVE LEFT: The Brightlingsea banner which now hangs in St James's Church in Victoria Place. RIGHT: These arms are carved on the back of a chair in All Saints Church, Brightlingsea. BELOW LEFT: The arms of the Dover Harbour Board, with which the Lord Warden was associated with the granting of their charter in 1606 by James I. RIGHT: Although not a member, the Yarmouth arms are an interesting variation of the Ports arms, three fish being used instead of three ships, perhaps to record the town's association with the Ports in the herring fair.

Of Note and Notoriety

The long roll call of the Lord Wardens of the Ports encompasses all kinds of men: great leaders who inspired the loyalty of the rough, tough, awkward seafaring men, nincompoops who treated the office as a mere sinecure, brave men and cowards, men of solid constancy and men of straw, men who were loyal both to the King and to their Portsmen and men who owed loyalty to none, and men who peformed all the duties and shouldered all the responsibilities without recourse to reliance on social status or the threat of punishment or appeal to higher authority, and mean men, timeservers, men who in their pride and arrogance sought to trample underfoot the pride and the chartered rights of Portsmen who were free men and no serfs.

They all left their marks, for good or ill, and though the works of many are swallowed up in the mists of time, the records of others survive to inspire, or to warn, those who follow.

There were great leaders of the Portsmen before the office of Lord Warden was created or formalised. Such a man was Godwin, Earl of the West Saxons and therefore of the lands of the Cinque Ports. A Saxon himself, he deplored, and struggled against, the increasing infiltration into the English court and society of courtiers and all kinds of place-seekers from Normandy, protecting the Englishmen he ruled, like for instance the men of Dover who had resisted Eustache, Earl of Boulogne, in his cynical disregard for an Englishman's rights of hearth and home, who went into exile because the King supported the foreign interloper and not Godwin's people. Godwin, forced into exile for a time, then returned home, came to the men he knew, the old Portsmen of the south-east coast, and inspired their loyalty. They rallied to him with their ships; the men of Hastings, of Pevensey, Dengeness, Romney, Hythe, Folkestone, Dover and Sandwich, sailed with him under his flag to London, where they proved more loyal to him than the Royal sailors did to the King.

Another such man was Hubert de Burgh. He was in personal charge of Dover Castle in 1216, inspiring his tiny garrison to hold out against a French besieging army many times the size and equipped with the latest siege equipment and engineers. In the following year the old soldier turned sailor and, having urgently mustered together twenty surviving ships from the Ports together with a few small supporting craft, he attacked and defeated an enemy fleet four times the size in the Straits of Dover, which was under the direction of Eustace the Monk, a most feared pirate and freebooter who often terrorised ships at sea.

An old record recounts how Hubert's men manoeuvred to windward of the enemy and then closed with them, pouring arrows into the enemy's ships, throwing clouds of quicklime into their faces and then carried out a classic Portsmens' assault technique, by ramming the enemy amidships, the metal sheathed prows of their ships cutting the enemy ships in half and sinking them.

The loyalty this man inspired was demonstrated when he fell foul of the King and found refuge in Brentwood. King Henry had him dragged out and ordered the blacksmith to put him in shackles. The blacksmith refused, telling the King 'I will die any death before I put iron on the man who freed England from the stranger and saved Dover from France'. There must have been something special about Hubert, who could inspire even a humble blacksmith to rebuke an all-powerful King.

John de Grey was in considerable disgrace when he held the offices of Governor of Dover Castle and Lord Warden in the reign of Henry III.

Athelmore, the King's half-brother, contrived to have himself appointed Bishop of Winchester, an appointment much opposed by the great barons. To secure his position he obtained ratification from the Pope, the papers of confirmation brought back to England by a friar, who landed unchallenged at Dover. Incensed at what they considered to be a grave dereliction of duty, the Portsmen sent their representative to Dover, who reproved the Lord Warden in the following terms:

'Have you been entrusted by the people of England, as a faithful Warden of the Cinque Ports, and you have suffered this person to hand without your knowledge, to the manifest violation of your oath? We think that you are not only unworthy of this place, but that you ought to be further questioned for so great a transgression'.

The final outcome of this affair is not known.

When Sir Robert de Burghersh was Lord Warden in the reign of Edward I there was, not for the first or the last time, serious trouble between the town of Faversham and the Abbot of Faversham Abbey, who at this time was Jeffery Bocton. He fined the barons of Faversham 500 Marks for usurping some Royal privileges the abbey claimed it held from the King. The exact details are obscure, but the abbot declared that the fine should be paid, but by instalments, £20 down and £15 a year.

Since, by their Cinque Ports charter, Portsmen were not to appear in courts outside the jurisdiction of the confederation the Warden, Robert, summoned the abbot to appear before him and when he did not do so, he arrested him and imprisoned him in Dover Castle.

Then the Archbishop took a hand and, hearing that the Lord Warden had imprisoned the abbot, he in turn summoned the Lord Warden to appear at his ecclesiastical court, but the Lord Warden, declining to do so, was condemned by process of the church to the penalty for contumacy.

Now the King himself became involved, since he was obviously not going to allow the Archbishop's claim to seniority over one of his most senior officers of state, and in the end the Archbishop was forced to submit.

This well illustrates the support and protection the individual members could receive from the Confederation, even when their adversary was one of the most powerful institutions in the mediaeval world. It also shows how the church endeavoured by every possible means to preserve every shred of its ancient power and privilege over the Ports who, one by one, were gradually divorcing themselves, as best they could, from their ancient thralldom.

But some Lord Wardens, far from emulating Sir Robert de Burghersh in their support of the Portsmen, actively offended them. Such a warden was Roger de Mortimer, Earl of March, a haughty and overbearing man who had no respect for the Portsmens' rights and privileges, treating them as mere serfs.

They, in turn, urgently sought the King's help and he responded, explaining in no uncertain terms the Portsmen's rights. His precept to the offending Warden reads as follows:

'Nevertheless, ye, and your officers, not having regard thereto, of late, by various processes, compel the Defendants to answer before you, not only at Shepway, and elsewhere, within your liberties, at your pleasure, by which means many of the inhabitants of the said Ports are highly aggrieved and disquieted, to the abatement of their conditions, and the manifest injury of their liberties and customs, and contrary to the Charters of our Grandfather and Father, and the custom of former times, for which we are humbly entreated to apply a suitable remedy. We, being unwilling that these Barons should be undeservedly oppressed, we command you, that, if the matter be so, you desist henceforth from such allurements, oppressions and vexations; and causing your officers wholly to desist, you permit the Mayors and Bailiffs of the Ports, to have and to hold, within their Ports, Pleas of Covenant, happening within their jurisdictions, without impediment or allurement made by you, aggreeable to the tenor of their Charters; and as they ought to have cognizance of this sort, and as the said Barons, and their ancestors, the aforesaid liberties, as well as before the making the aforesaid Charters and Confirmations, as since, have been accustomed reasonably to use and enjoy, we command the distresses which have been taken for the Barons' Causes, from any of the said Barons, to be restored; and we direct to all who are Complainants before you in such matters, to go to the Ports, or Port, in which they say the trespass was committed, there to receive justice from the Mayors and Bailiffs of those places, as it ought to be done'.

From this it will be seen that, not only could the Portsmen have support from the Lord Warden against a quarrelsome ecclesiastic, but that they could also obtain support from the King against an erring Lord Warden.

A notable Lord Warden was Prince Henry, who later became King Henry VIII.

Both when as a prince he was Lord Warden, and later when he was King, Henry spent much time in the Ports, and there are instances of his enjoyment of the company of the old Portsmen. Among other things, he did many tests and experiments with the new guns then becoming important weapons both for defence and offence in warfare, and his test firings from Archcliffe Fort in Dover established him as one of the foremost experts in the use of gunpowder of his day.

It was from one of the head ports, Dover that, accompanied by his own naval contingent and the Portsmens' ships, he sailed for the meeting of the Field of the Cloth of Gold.

He was familiar with the shipbuilding activities of the Ports, particularly with that of Rye, and it is thought that some of the craftsmen from Rye helped to build the ship he commissioned at Smallhythe, then the port of Tenterden. He took a personal interest in this ship and rode down from London to oversee its construction.

His pioneer interest in the use of guns, both ashore and afloat, his encourgement of the building of bigger, specially designed and constructed ships for his new and expanding navy, and the development of new methods of war at sea, made the small multi-purpose Cinque Ports ships less and less valuable for naval operations.

Arthur Plantagenet, Viscount Lisle, a natural son of Edward IV, was somewhat unfortunate. As Lord Warden he was involved in operations with the Cinque Ports ships when he was shipwrecked, running on rocks near Brest. He was then appointed Lieutenant Governor of Calais where, for some reason, his loyalty was suspect and he was brought home and imprisoned in the Tower.

When he came up for trial his innocence was fully established and he was immediately released, receiving from Henry VIII a 'gracious message, together with a diamond ring'.

Whether it was the strain of the trial, the sudden acquittal, or the subsequent celebrations, is not known, but he died from a heart attack almost immediately.

From the Restoration, beginning with the appointment of James, Duke of York, who afterwards became James II, the posts of Governor of the Castle, Lord Warden and Admiral of the Cinque Ports, became a sinecure filled by members of the aristorcracy and high society who understood little, and it seems cared less, about the real nature of their committments to these once great offices of state.

Several eminent men however came to office at the end of the 18th century and in the 19th century. William Pitt, the Prime Minister, was appointed in 1793 and served for 13 years, being the last holder of the post to make the necessary naval and military decisions for the defence of the country against the threat of invasion, this time against Napoleon, whose massed invasion forces were assembled on the beaches of Boulogne. Pitt also organised a defence force drawn from the Cinque Ports and their limbs, and indeed became one of those Cinque Ports volunteers himself. He spent as much time as he could spare, from his governmental responsibilities in London, on the Kent coast, where he occupied the Lord Warden's official residence, Walmer Castle. At sea, the fleet under Nelson then performed the task of policing the narrow seas as their forerunner, the Cinque Ports fleet, had done for so many earlier centuries.

The last Lord Warden to exercise any real authority was the Duke of Wellington, who took his responsibilities seriously, living in Walmer Castle for much of each year. In his long period of service, from 1829 to 1852, he discharged the social and legal duties which remained attached to the office, all of them with care and precision, occupying the Lord Warden's seat in the hall on the south side of the nave of old St James's Church in Dover, supervising the sessions of the Lord Warden's courts of Chancery, Admiralty and the pilots' court of Lodemanage, all of which ceased to function after his death, their work transferred to other institutions.

After the 1939-45 war the two great men, both of them intimately involved in its victory, who occupied the office were Sir Winston Churchill, and Sir Robert Menzies.

Our present Constable of Dover Castle, Lord Warden and Admiral of the Cinque Ports, that gracious lady,, H M Queen Elizabeth the Queen Mother, is the Royal holder of an ancient office held in earlier times by other distinguished members of the Royal family.

A drawing of Queenborough Castle, now completely disappeared, the official residence of the Lord Warden in earlier times.

ABOVE: A Hogarth drawing of Queenborough, which lost two of its former features to the Ports: the Wool Staple, and the Lord Warden's official residence. CENTRE: Walmer Castle was made the Warden's official residence in the early years of the 18th century. BELOW: This lake in the garden of the Harbour-master's house at Smallhythe was the dock in which Henry VIII's ships were built. It was excavated a few years ago.

136

ABOVE: The old harbourmaster's house at Smallhythe, near Tenterden, now the Ellen Terry Museum. Henry VIII came to inspect his ship being built here. BELOW: An interior view of the gracious living quarters in Walmer Castle.

HRH Queen Elizabeth the Queen Mother inspects
the naval guard of honour at her 1979 Royal Court of
Shepway.

Bibliography

The materials available for the study of the history of the Cinque Ports are voluminous and widely spread over a number of institutions, libraries and museums. However a good starting point must be the reference sections of the public libraries in the Cinque Port towns themselves and in the appropriate district and county headquarters.

From the public libraries also access can be gained to the many standard works of one kind or another. A selection of these is:

Camden's Britannica, for Surrey and Sussex, and for Kent.
Villare Cantianum. Philepot.
The Sussex County Magazine. Various issues.
The History of Kent. Hasted.
The History of Kent. Ireland.
Chambers Encyclopaedia has useful articles.
A Short History of the English People. Old but detailed.
The Victoria County Histories for Kent, Essex and Sussex.
Archaeologia Cantiana. Libraries hold indices.
Transactions of the Sussex Archaeological Society.
Archaeological Review.
A Calendar of the White and Black Books of the Cinque Ports. Hull.
Historic Towns. Cinque Ports. Burrows.
The Cinque Ports. Bavington Jones.
The Grand Court of Shepway. Knocker.
The Cinque Ports. Jessup.
Constitutional History of the Cinque Ports. Murray.
The Saxon Shore. Mothersole.
Kent and the Cinque Ports. Boorman.
Collections for a history of Sandwich in Kent. Boys.
History of Deal. Laker.
Historic Hastings. Baines.
History of the Town and Port of Fordwich. Woodruffe.
History of Sandwich. Bentwich.
History, of the Castle, Town and Port of Dover. Statham.
Old Tenderden. Mace.
A history of the town and Port of Romney.
History of Winchelsea. Cooper.
History of Dover Castle. Darrell.
History of the Town of Brightlingsea. Dickin.
The Liberty of Brightlingsea. Dove.
Folkestone. The Story of a Town. Bishop
Hythe Haven. Forbes.

There is a good selection of local history matter at the Fleur De Lis Heritage Centre, Faversham, Kent.

A quantity of useful material in MSS form, in the reference section of the Seaford Public Library, is also available.

Index

140

Subscribers

Presentation Copies

1 HM Queen Elizabeth the Queen Mother, Lord Warden of the Cinque Ports
2 Ian Gill LLB, Registrar & Seneschal, Cinque Ports
3 Kent County Library
4 East Sussex County Library
5 Dover District Council
6 Hastings Borough Council
7 Hythe Town Council
8 Rye Town Council
9 Folkestone Charter Trustees

10 Ivan & Margaret Green
11 Clive & Carolyn Birch
12 H.W. Sneller
13 Mrs Audrey Hickson
14 D.A. Leach
15 Mr & Mrs J.H. White
16 D.J. Kettle
17 Cllr. Mrs M. Hart
18
19 F.H. Hart
20 Mr & Mrs H.J. Lavers
21 Miss O. May
22 Mrs G. Lee-Marson
23 C. Ovenden
24 Mrs Iris Dean
25 Mr & Mrs Fowell
26 Mrs Margaret Green
27 Mr & Mrs Dennis Green
28 Mrs S. Corrall
29
31 Mrs Dorothy Jeffery
32 W.G.J. Bates
33 Mr & Mrs J.W.I. Newman
34 Mr & Mrs A.R. Fynn
35 Mrs E. Beacroft
36 Michael John Sharp
37 Maurice Charles
   Morecroft
38 Mary & Richard Hoskins
39 George William Mold
40 John Russell Taylor
41 G.H. Coulter
42 Mr & Mrs J.D. Pascall
43 Mr & Mrs K.M. Pascall
44 R.E. King
45 E.H. King
46 F.A. Newenham
47
49 Mrs D.M. Benefield
50 Mrs Elsie V. Williams
51 J. Wilsher
52 M.S. Whitehead
53 Frederick J. Simpson
54 Mrs Joan Scott
55 Mrs Edna Cockram

56 Mrs Eileen Curtis
57 Mrs M.E. Warren
58 N.E. Pott
59
60 Norman E.P. King
61 Mr & Mrs P. Newton
62 Mr & Mrs L.R.
   Williamson
63 Miss M.A. Bowden
64 Dr & Mrs R.S. Stevens
65 Mr & Mrs T.F. Stevens
66 Mr & Mrs R.G. Grace
67 Mr & Mrs L. Ashton
68 Mrs M.A. Atherton
69 Miss Hazel Hughes
70 Mrs E.M.A. Pain
71 A. Doolin
72 Miss M.F. Bones
73 Miss K.E. Goodfellow
74 Lillian Kay
75 Mr & Mrs W.W.R. Husk
76 Dover Museum
77 J. Le Prevost
78 W.E. Pine
79 E.E. Rogers
80 G.W. Ledger
81 P. Dunning
82 Mrs B.F. Smith
83 P.G. Bloom
84 Mrs J. Tyson
85 Miss E. Burbeck
86 Mrs J.I. Davies
87 Anthony Graham Belsey
88 Mrs Hazle Norris
89 F.P. Delahaye
90 R.C. Chatburn
91 J.G. Harman
92 Ray Warner
93 Mr & Mrs R.D. Dixon
94 Sybil Standing
95 Mr & Mrs Welby
96 P.G. Henneker
97 Mr & Mrs W.H. Hopper
98 V. Hoffmeyer
99 M.A. Pascall

100 M. May
101 D. Donovan
102 R.P. Friend
103 John Blay
104 Lee Gillham
105 Cllr. Mrs M. Hart
106 I.B. Cook JP
107 Mrs M.A. Ryeland
108 L.W. Gibbs
109 P. Newman
110 Mrs E.J. Tomlin
111 The Downs C.E. Primary
   School, Walmer
112 Mrs M. Underdown
113 Allan Kime
114 Peter Kime
115 A.R. & P.E. Gay
116 Mr & Mrs G.E. Saddleton
117 Miss E.A. Saddleton
118 C.J. Grant
119 Claude Harcout
   Conybeare
120 R.C. Page
121 E. Kanzler
122 Alan W. Rainsley
123 Frank Mathews
124 Malcolm Pratt
125 D.V. Henderson
126 Mrs J.A. Limb
127 Douglas E. Sturrock
128 David A. Cook
129 David Wood
130 Alexander Wood
131 Hugh V. Roberts
132 S.G. Brown
133 Tenterden Town
   Council
134 Alan R.F. Moore
135 Ralph Ronald Brand
136 Sir Percy Rugg
137 Canon David Naumann
138 Frank Abbott
139 Henry Edwards
140 Scilla Greenfield
141 Kenneth Downe

END PAPERS: FRONT — Walmer Castle in the early
years of the 19th century. Drawn by J. Wright and
dedicated to the Prime Minister and Lord Warden of
the Cinque Ports. BACK — An old etching at the
beach at Great Yarmouth, the site of the old Herring
Fair.